POLITICS
IN A
PLURALIST
DEMOCRACY

Studies of Voting in the 1960 Election

By LUCY S. DAWIDOWICZ
and LEON J. GOLDSTEIN

With a Foreword by
RICHARD M. SCAMMON, Director, Bureau of the Census

GREENWOOD PRESS, PUBLISHERS
WESTPORT, CONNECTICUT

Library of Congress Cataloging in Publication Data

Dawidowicz, Lucy S
   Politics in a pluralist democracy.

   Reprint of the ed. published by the Institute of
Human Relations Press.
   Includes bibliographical references.
    1.   Presidents--United States--Election--1960.
I. Goldstein, Leon J., joint author. II. Title.
[JK526 1960.D32]   329'.023'730921   74-9630
ISBN 0-8371-7599-2

Originally published in 1963 by Institute of Human Relations
Press, New York

Reprinted with the permission of Institute of Human Relations-
The American Jewish Committee

Reprinted in 1974 by Greenwood Press,
a division of Williamhouse-Regency Inc.

Library of Congress Catalog Card Number 74-9630

ISBN 0-8371-7599-2

Printed in the United States of America

CONTENTS

Acknowledgments ix

Foreword by Richard M. Scammon xi

Introduction 3

MULTI-ETHNIC CITIES

   1. Boston 9

   2. Buffalo 16

   3. Cincinnati 22

   4. Providence 28

   5. Los Angeles 35

THE RELIGIOUS ISSUE IN RURAL AREAS

   6. Fundamentalists: Tennessee, Illinois, Ohio 41

   7. French Catholics, Anglo-American Protestants
      and Negroes: Louisiana 49

   8. Lutheran and Catholic Counties: Minnesota 51

JEWISH VOTING BEHAVIOR

   9. Suburbs and Near-Suburbs 61

   10. Special Appeals to Jewish Voters 71

   11. The Jewish Liberal Tradition 76

Concluding Observations 91

Index 98

LIST OF TABLES

1. Democratic Vote in Selected Predominantly Irish
   Precincts in Boston, 1956-1960   11

2. Democratic Vote in Selected Non-Irish Precincts
   in Boston, 1956-1960   12

3. Democratic Vote and Deviations from the Democratic
   Norm in Presidential Elections in Buffalo, 1952-1960   19

4. Democratic Vote in Three Wards in Cincinnati,
   1952-1960   24

5. Deviations from the Democratic Norm in Four
   Elections in Cincinnati, 1952-1960   26

6. Democratic Vote in Five Predominantly Italian Ward
   Districts in Providence, 1952-1960   30

7. Major Ethnic Groups in Three Upper-income State
   Representative Districts in Providence, 1954   33

8. Democratic and Republican Vote in Three Upper-
   income State Representative Districts with
   Greatest Yankee Concentration in Providence, 1960   33

9. Presidential Preferences, by Religion, in California,
   1960   35

10. Democratic Vote in Negro and Mexican Districts
    in Los Angeles, 1952-1960   37

11. Democratic Share of Major-party Vote for President
    in Eleven Tennessee Counties, 1944-1960   43

12. Democratic Vote for President and Governor in
    Three Downstate Illinois Counties, 1928-1960   45

13. Democratic Vote for President in Six Southern
    Ohio Counties, 1928-1960   47

14. Democratic Vote for Senator, Governor, and President
    in Six Southern Ohio Counties, 1956-1960   48

15. Democratic Vote in Ten Predominantly Lutheran
    Counties in Minnesota, 1928-1932, 1948-1960   53

16. Democratic Vote in Six Predominantly Catholic
    Counties in Minnesota, 1928, 1932, 1948-1960   56

17. Republican Vote in Ward 50 and Chicago, 1950-1956   62

18. Democratic Vote in Ward 50 and Chicago, 1960   63

19. Democratic Vote for President in Selected Jewish
    and Scandinavian Precincts in Ward 50,
    Chicago, 1956 and 1960   63

20. Democratic Vote in Jewish and Other Precincts
    of Chicago Suburbs, 1960   64

21. Democratic Vote in Precincts 70 to 80 Per Cent Jewish,
    by Economic Rank, in and near Chicago, 1960   65

22. 1960 Presidential Choice and 1956 Presidential
    Vote, by Religion, in Two Detroit Suburbs   69

23. Presidential Choices in 1960 Democratic Primary,
    by Religion, in Oak Park   70

ACKNOWLEDGMENTS

As an intergroup-relations agency, the American Jewish Committee has for many years paid close attention to the group aspects of American politics. Partly this has been a practical need — to refute uninformed or fallacious charges of something sinister called bloc voting, as supposedly practiced by Jews, or Catholics, or Negroes, or foreigners of one sort or another. Almost at every election, the Committee finds it necessary to inform editors and commentators, and sometimes politicians, that religious, ethnic, or racial groups are not subject to the political control and discipline of some central authority and that the votes of the members of such groups cannot be "delivered." On the other hand, the Committee often has to remind people who deny bloc voting that its absence does not mean the absence of group influences. Just as a citizen's family, class, occupation, education, region, and friendships affect his political attitudes and behavior, so do the traditions, values, and needs associated with his membership in a religious, ethnic, or racial group.

Another part of the Committee's interest in the relation between group membership and politics has been more theoretical. Politics, and especially elections, put group life and intergroup relations under a strong light. An examination of those phenomena in a political context is bound to deepen our understanding of them. When the Committee, with a grant from the Lilly Endowment, sponsored a Conference on Group Life in America in 1956, the papers and discussions gave due weight to politics, as one can see by referring to those conference papers that were published in the "Ethnic Groups in American Life" issue of *Daedalus* (Spring 1961). Again in 1956, the Committee asked Moses Rischin, then a staff member, to study the group factors in the presidential campaign and election of that year. His analysis was later published in condensed form by the Center for the Study of Democratic Institutions of the Fund for the Republic, as *"Our Own Kind": Voting by Race, Creed, or National Origin*. The campaign and election of 1960, with an Irish Catholic as one of the candidates, promised to be especially instructive. It was our good fortune to be asked to do that research.

All our colleagues at the American Jewish Committee to whom we turned for help or advice were unfailingly interested and helpful, and it is an especially pleasant obligation to express our thanks to them. In particular, David Danzig, associate director of the American Jewish Committee, and Milton Himmelfarb, director of its Jewish Information Service, encouraged us by their enthusiasm, helped us by their guidance, and influenced our thinking by their ideas about group life in America; Roy Millenson gave us much useful information; Benjamin B. Ringer patiently helped us in our statistical problems, and George Salomon edited the successive drafts painstakingly and critically. Morris Fine, on behalf of the Institute of Human Relations Press, guided the production of the book.

These studies could not have been prepared without the kind assistance of many people with expert knowledge and understanding of particular communities or regions. Acknowledgment of our indebtedness to each of them appears in the appropriate chapter. In addition, we are grateful to Dr. William R. Prendergast, research director of the Republican National Committee, and to two New York Democrats, Mr. Julius S. S. Edelstein and Judge Millard Midonick. We also thank the library of the National Municipal League.

The final responsibility, of course, is ours.

L.S.D.   L.J.G.

The American Jewish Committee
New York, N. Y.
July, 1963

FOREWORD

In recent years the "maturing" of American politics has been the theme of a number of political essays. As we move more completely into a suburb-oriented affluent society, as immigration restrictions limit the influx of other peoples, and as ease of communications and travel knit our national life ever closer, our politics takes on a new, bland, conforming character. At least, that is the general thrust of the "maturity" premise.

This study of religion and ethnic origin and the effects of these factors on the 1960 Presidential election highlights a number of unbland and non-conforming aspects of our political behavior. When taken with the vitally important factors of family political inheritance and personal economic status, the concept of "blandification" becomes more a hypothesis than an acceptable definition of today's developing American politics.

As the scholar faces the mass of material presently available for studies of these American politics he must react much as a youngster in a candy store. There is so much at hand—survey research, elections data, Census studies—it becomes difficult to know where to begin. In this volume the authors make such a beginning with five American cities, and this kind of study may hopefully be expected to lead to comparable research undertakings for many other urban areas.

But rural areas are not neglected either, nor should they be. In 1960 some of the most striking examples of religious and ethnic influence could be obtained from the voting behavior of rural areas. Though America is becoming more and more urban each day, farm and small-town voting patterns are a vital part of any total effort to understand modern-day American political operations. The contrast between farm and non-farm rural voting in a state like Minnesota makes an intriguing study, and the correlation of religious belief with voting patterns in the rural counties of Wisconsin illumines some striking aspects of our political life.

Perhaps as fascinating as any in electoral statistical analysis is the enquiry into non-conforming patterns. Study of the voting patterns of 1956 will reveal an over-all bettering of the Republican position vis-a-vis 1962. But important to any understanding of the Eisenhower era is the examination of election figures and survey research materials in those states in which the 1956 Eisenhower vote ran *behind* that of 1952.

Equally, in 1960, the basic issues of the nation's last Presidential campaign seem much clearer when the statistics are considered with respect to the areas in which Mr. Nixon actually polled better in 1960 than had President Eisenhower in 1956. Despite the general national move towards the Democratic side, there were many counties in which the trend was just the reverse—and the listing of these counties underlines the religious issue as it developed in some parts of the country.

Studies of this type may well increase. They should, for analysis of our political behavior by a combination of survey research and election-day voter behavior seems more and more to be the most helpful way in which to try to interpret the workings of our democracy. The authors and the American Jewish Committee are to be congratulated for undertaking this very useful work.

RICHARD M. SCAMMON
Director
Bureau of the Census

Politics in a Pluralist Democracy

INTRODUCTION

THE point of departure for the studies which follow is our interest in ethnic and religious influences upon voting as a significant aspect of American intergroup relations. Ten years ago Samuel Lubell underscored the importance of the ethnic factor in American political life, showing that dichotomies—such as liberalism-conservatism or isolationism-internationalism—which are often attributed to differences in class, region or ideology were also, perhaps primarily, expressions of ethnic interests, disagreements or conflicts.[1] Likewise, a number of studies (some of them mentioned in the next section) have recognized that religion is a factor of some relevance to political behavior. Yet little serious attention has been paid to religious[2] or ethnic affiliation as influences in the development of political traditions. Such traditions deserve more serious treatment than they have usually received, but we do not begin to probe their importance in politics unless we advance beyond the customary attempts to determine the mutual tolerance of Protestants, Catholics and Jews.

Research to Date

The study of elections in the United States is comparatively new; serious investigation began only in 1928, with the publication of Stuart A. Rice's *Quantitative Methods in Politics*.[3] The presidential election of 1928 was studied by William F. Ogburn and Nell S. Talbot in their classical monograph on the roles of prohibition and Al Smith's Catholicism,[4] as well as by Roy V. Peel and Thomas C. Donnelly in their pioneer study *The 1928 Campaign*.[5] Since then research on voting has expanded and has adopted

---

[1] Samuel Lubell, *The Future of American Politics* (New York: Harper & Bros., 1952).

[2] A recent noteworthy exception is Gerhard Lenski, *The Religious Factor* (Garden City, N.Y.: Doubleday & Co., 1961).

[3] See Peter H. Rossi, "Four Landmarks in Voting Research," in Eugene Burdick and Arthur J. Brodbeck, eds., *American Voting Behavior* (Glencoe, Ill.: Free Press, 1960).

[4] W. F. Ogburn and N. S. Talbot, "A Measurement of the Factors in the Presidential Election of 1928," *Social Forces*, VIII (1929), 175-183.

[5] Roy Victor Peel and Thomas C. Donnelly, *The 1928 Campaign, An Analysis* (New York: R. R. Smith, 1931).

a variety of methods and resources, drawn from political science, history, psychology (particularly attitude research) and sociology (particularly public-opinion research and ecology).[6]

Political scientists pioneered in applying historical techniques to the study of voting, by analyzing voting statistics for long periods in the context of political developments, economic trends and particular local, state or regional conditions. V. O. Key has been the outstanding scholar in this area. His books and studies on local, state and regional politics have become standards in the field.

Attitude research involves the use of surveys to analyze representative national, local or group samples of voters. Data are gathered through interviews covering political attitudes and opinions as well as actual voting. The dimensions of time and change have been added through the so-called panel technique, under which the same persons are interviewed several times. This technique was pioneered by Paul F. Lazarsfeld and Columbia University's Bureau of Applied Social Research, in two intensive studies of single communities and their institutions: one on the presidential election of 1940 in Erie County, Ohio,[7] the other on that of 1948 in Elmira, New York.[8] The Survey Research Center of the University of Michigan has applied the panel technique on a national scale relying heavily on quantitative methods and statistics. The Center's study of the 1960 presidential election[9] was based on a series of five panel interviews, begun in 1956 with 1,500 respondents (a number later reduced by death and other causes). Voting figures, together with data on such factors as occupation, schooling,

[6]G. Dupeux, "Electoral Behavior" (English summary of "Le Comportement électoral"), *Current Sociology* (UNESCO), III (1954-55), 4; Louis Harris, "Some Observations on Election Behavior Research," *Public Opinion Quarterly*, XX (1956), 379-391.

[7]Paul F. Lazarsfeld and others, *The People's Choice* (New York: Duell, Sloan & Pearce, 1944; Columbia University Press, 1948).

[8]Bernard E. Berelson, Paul F. Lazarsfeld and William N. McPhee, *Voting: A Study of Opinion Formation in a Presidential Campaign* (Chicago: University of Chicago Press, 1954).

[9]Philip E. Converse, Angus Campbell, Warren E. Miller and Donald Stokes, "Stability and Change in 1960: A Reinstating Election," *American Political Science Review*, LV (1961), 269-280. Professor Miller was kind enough to make this study available to us before publication.

religious affiliation, normal political preferences or attitudes, and exposure to mass media, were analyzed with the help of advanced statistical theory and data-processing machines. The study concluded that Kennedy's religion had been the most decisive issue and had cost him 1.5 million votes.

Ecological research has related the social, economic, religious and ethnic characteristics of people in small electoral units to the way they vote. This type of inquiry has been developed chiefly by students of public opinion and journalists interested in predicting the outcome of elections. Samuel Lubell and Louis Harris have been the chief practitioners; unfortunately, most of Harris's studies are not generally available.

With the broadening interest of scholars in metropolitan problems, the socio-cultural influences on political life and voting are now beginning to receive more attention. For example, the recent studies in politics prepared under the direction of Edward W. Banfield (issued by the Joint Center for Urban Studies of the Massachusetts Institute of Technology and Harvard University) show considerable sensitivity to ethnic and religious factors. Historians, also, looking backward at American politics, place increasing emphasis on socio-cultural differences and their role in political organization and conflict.[10]

Selection of Areas for the Present Studies

In 1960 the candidacy of John F. Kennedy, an Irish Catholic, offered an opportunity to study group behavior and intergroup relations in a political context. For this purpose we selected different religious and ethnic groups in a variety of cities and regions. Before we could speak with any degree of confidence about the voting tendencies within a given group, we had to find members of that group in sufficient concentration—a task which has become difficult since urban renewal and migration to the suburbs have hastened the erosion of long-established ethnic neighborhoods. In some communities today it is almost impossible to find election units, however small, with homogeneous populations.

----

[10]E. g., Lee Benson, *The Concept of Jacksonian Democracy: New York as a Test Case* (Princeton, N. J.: Princeton University Press, 1961).

Our final selection of cities and regions included Boston, Providence and Buffalo, for their large numbers of Irish, Italian and Polish voters, respectively;[11] portions of Tennessee, Ohio and southern Illinois for Fundamentalist Protestants; and Cincinnati for German Catholics. In addition we compared Protestants with Catholics in Louisiana as well as rural Minnesota and studied how Jews voted in various urban and suburban places. Within cities or regions we usually singled out smaller subdivisions where one or another group predominates heavily. Our ethnic, racial and religious characterizations of areas are based on Federal and church censuses, on lists of registered voters and on a variety of local studies.

Available data differ markedly from place to place. Lists of voters are useful for determining the ethnic homogeneity of an area, and we used them where we could. Demographic and economic information may be scanty, or it may be plentiful—either in the form of a published study (such as we used for Providence) or in the files of local experts (as we discovered during our study of Detroit suburbs). Data of this kind must be gathered in more and more communities and made generally available, if the political behavior of Americans is to be better understood.[12]

---

[11]Throughout, "Irish" should be understood as a shorthand term for "Americans of Irish descent," "Italians" for "Americans of Italian descent," etc.

[12]Cf. Louis Harris, "The Relation of Polling Data to Analyses of Election Results in Explaining Political Behavior," *Public Opinion Quarterly*, XIX (1955), 316-319, and *idem*, "Some Observations on Election Behavior Research," *ibid.*, XX (1956), 380-383.

Multi-Ethnic Cities

1. BOSTON

BOSTON* is a Democratic stronghold. Eisenhower never won it, though he took Massachusetts twice; in 1952 the city gave Stevenson nearly 60 per cent of its vote, and in 1956 somewhat over 54 per cent. But a still more important fact of Boston's political life is that for a long time a majority of the city's people have been Irish Catholics.[1] Citizens of Italian, Jewish and Yankee Protestant background tend to identify the Irish with the notorious Democratic machine that has become almost synonymous with Boston's government, and generally hold a low opinion of local politics. Yet, except for the Yankee Protestants, whom the Irish supplanted as the ruling group several generations ago, the various minorities did not turn whatever anti-Irish resentment they felt into a vote against Kennedy in 1960.

Kennedy won almost 75 per cent of the vote in Boston. The evidence indicates that voters in largely Italian and Jewish precincts, far from resenting him as an Irishman, supported him even more strongly than the city as a whole. Possibly, Jewish voters found the liberal internationally-minded urban Kennedy an appealing candidate; and possibly the Italians, engaged in improving their own status in America, were especially sensitive to the religious issue. But whatever the merit of these suppositions, which would be equally applicable in other parts of the country, it must also be remembered that on his native grounds Kennedy has been a highly unusual phenomenon—indeed, the most popular political figure—for a number of years.

In 1952, the year Eisenhower won Massachusetts with more than 54 per cent of the vote, Kennedy took a Senate seat from the Republican incumbent, Henry Cabot Lodge. By 1958, when he was up for reelection, the Republicans had so despaired of defeating him that they ran only a perfunctory campaign with a little-known candidate, Vincent J. Celeste; this time Kennedy

---

*For data and advice we owe thanks to Samuel Katz, regional director of the American Jewish Committee, Professor Murray B. Levin of Boston University, and Professor Moses Rischin of the University of California at Los Angeles.

[1]For a good brief account, see Murray B. Levin, *The Alienated Voter: Politics in Boston* (New York: Holt, Rinehart and Winston, 1960).

9

polled more than 73 per cent of the state's vote, and more than 84 per cent of the city's. In the 1960 election the Kennedy vote in Boston was about 10 per cent less than in 1958—in part, no doubt, because the Republicans were now making a serious effort.

The present study covers selected precincts in nine of Boston's 22 wards. Five of these nine areas are predominantly Irish; their socio-economic characteristics and voting records from 1956 to 1960 are given in Table 1.[2] As the figures show, the Boston Irish are quite steadfast in their devotion to the Democratic party. Except in the high-income 20th Ward, there was hardly any difference between the percentage of the vote for Furcolo in the 1958 gubernatorial race and that for Kennedy in the presidential election two years later. The 20th, as might be expected, is generally the least Democratic of the five wards, but even here Democratic candidates more often than not roll up substantial majorities. The Irish precincts' adherence to the Democratic party was weakest in the 1956 presidential vote; the turnout for Stevenson fell considerably below that for Furcolo, the candidate for Governor, and in the 20th Ward precincts a majority voted for Eisenhower.

Voting records of the four non-Irish neighborhoods studied are reported in Table 2. One of the four, Ward 5, is a part of the famous Beacon Hill-Back Bay section. The returns from this high-status Yankee Protestant stronghold testify to Kennedy's extraordinary attractiveness for Bostonians; normally about two-thirds Republican, the area gave him a majority in 1958, and 42 per cent of its vote in 1960.

Two other sections studied are normally Democratic: a Jewish area in Dorchester with low-middle to middle incomes, and a predominantly Italian low-to-middle-income district in East Boston. In 1960 the Jewish precincts departed from their norm by giving the Democratic senatorial candidate, Thomas J. O'Connor, Jr., less than 60 per cent of their support. But O'Connor ran behind the other major Democratic nominees in most of the areas studied and in the state as a whole—probably because his oppo-

---

[2]Ethnic and income characterizations of Boston wards are from Levin, *op. cit.*, pp. 78-80.

TABLE 1
DEMOCRATIC VOTE IN SELECTED PREDOMINANTLY IRISH PRECINCTS IN BOSTON, 1956-1960
(Per cent)

Election	Ward 2 (Charleston) Precincts 2, 3, 4, 7	Ward 13 (Dorchester) Precincts 1, 3, 4, 5, 10	Ward 15 (Dorchester) Precincts 3, 4, 6, 10	Ward 16 (Dorchester) Precincts 1, 4, 5, 9	Ward 20 (Roxbury) Precincts 6, 7, 8, 11*
	Low income	Low to middle income	Middle income	Middle income slightly above Ward 15 precincts	Upper and upper-middle income
1956: President Stevenson (D) Eisenhower (R)	67.8	55.2	58.0	53.6	38.8
1956: Governor Furcolo (D) Whittier (R)	80.8	73.1	77.1	62.2	57.0
1958: Senator Kennedy (D) Celeste (R)	94.4	88.0	91.2	87.2	81.7
1958: Governor Furcolo (D) Gibbons (R)	88.0	78.4	83.4	82.6	63.8
1960: President Kennedy (D) Nixon (R)	89.4	78.8	82.4	82.9	69.9
1960: Senator O'Connor (D) Saltonstall (R)	76.3	62.4	65.7	64.0	48.2
1960: Governor Ward ((D) Volpe (R)	80.9	65.0	69.1	69.0	51.9

*These four precincts, though predominantly Irish, are ethnically more mixed than the rest.
Source: Computed from election returns published in the Boston *Globe*, November 7, 1956; November 5, 1958; November 9, 1960.

TABLE 2

DEMOCRATIC VOTE IN SELECTED
NON-IRISH PRECINCTS IN BOSTON, 1956-1960

(Per cent)

Election	Ward 1 (East Boston) Precincts 1, 7, 8, 12 Italian, low to middle income	Ward 5 (Beacon Hill) and Back Bay) Precincts 3, 4, 6, 9 Yankee, middle and upper-middle income	Ward 12 (Roxbury) Precincts 3, 5, 6, 8 Negro, low to low-middle income	Ward 14 (Dorchester) Precincts 2, 3, 10, 11 Jewish, low-middle to middle income
1956: President Stevenson (D) vs. Eisenhower (R)	57.8	33.5	49.4	78.6
1956: Governor Furcolo (D) vs. Whittier (R)	80.8	35.4	59.2	80.0
1958: Senator Kennedy (D) vs. Celeste (R)	86.5	54.4	81.4	90.4
1958: Governor Furcolo (D) vs. Gibbons (R)	85.5	36.7	68.8	80.4
1960: President Kennedy (D) vs. Nixon (R)	84.6	42.1	55.2	77.4
1960: Senator O'Connor (D) vs. Saltonstall (R)	58.8	29.7	41.7	58.9
1960: Governor Ward (D) vs. Volpe (R)	56.4	26.0	46.0	60.6

Source: Computed from election returns published in the Boston *Globe*, November 7, 1956;
November 5, 1958; November 9, 1960.

nent was the incumbent, Leverett Saltonstall, a respected member of his party's leadership in the Senate and a moderate with a good record. In the same election, the Italian precincts favored the Democratic candidate for Governor, Joseph D. Ward, even though the opposing Republican was an Italian, John R. Volpe. Ward's majority was relatively small, because some voters crossed party lines for the sake of a fellow Italian, but such crossing over was far less pronounced than among Italians in Providence (see pp. 31-32).[3]

The most unexpected results were those from a low- to low-middle-income district in Roxbury, inhabited chiefly by Negroes as well as some Jews and others. These precincts usually support Democratic candidates, though they rolled up a bare majority for Eisenhower in 1956. In the senatorial election of 1956 Kennedy won more than 81 per cent of the area's vote. Yet in 1960 the precincts gave him a majority almost 20 per cent below that in the city as a whole and favored the Republican candidates for Senator and Governor.

A well-informed observer consulted in the course of this study suggests an explanation. Negroes in Boston are generally apathetic about politics; before each election the local staff of the National Association for the Advancement of Colored People must stir up their interest and persuade them to register and vote. Since the sympathies of the staff tend to be with the Democrats, that party usually benefits. In 1960, however, the Boston NAACP found itself in financial difficulties so grave as to threaten the existence of the organization, and the energies of its staff had to be concentrated on fund raising. Our observer believes that the absence of NAACP's usual effort accounts in part for the poor Democratic showing among the Negroes of the 12th Ward.

---

[3]Murray B. Levin and George Blackwood have argued in *The Compleat Politician* (Indianapolis and New York: The Bobbs-Merrill Co., 1962), chapter II, that the shift of the Italian vote was one of the factors in Ward's defeat, but it is clear from the authors' account of the 1960 gubernatorial campaign that Volpe's Italian descent was only one of the reasons why his fellow ethnics voted for him. That such a shift is less automatic here than in Providence is plainly suggested by the same Italian voters' failure to support Celeste against Kennedy in 1958.

Ralph Otwell[4] confirms that Boston Negroes are politically passive, powerless and unorganized. He adds that in presidential elections the Democratic party has been losing ground among Boston Negroes since 1948; in 1956, for example, Stevenson polled 70 to 75 per cent of the Negro vote in the nation as a whole, but only 55 per cent in Boston, while the Democratic candidate for Governor simultaneously won 63 per cent of the Boston Negro vote. Our findings show the same trend: as we have seen, the Negro voters of the 12th Ward liked Kennedy as the senatorial candidate in 1958 more than as the presidential candidate in 1960.

Still another important fact about the 1960 election is that a Negro, Edward W. Brooke, who had built up a political organization during the previous decade, was the Republican candidate for Secretary of State. Brooke did not win, but he received almost 1.1 million of the 2.3 million votes cast. There can be little doubt that the prominent appearance of a Negro on the Republican ticket—not a common occurrence in any state or either major party—had some effect upon Negro voters, since for minority groups "the pursuit of elected public office is an important aspect of the struggle for equality of acceptance."[5] Actually, the Brooke organization proved very successful; for the first time, a Negro Republican, A. S. Brothers of the 12th Ward, was elected to the state's House of Representatives.

Brooke's effect on the voters of the 12th Ward is clearly indicated by a comparison of the 1958 and 1960 returns for Secretary of State. In 1958 the Democratic candidate easily carried the ward, with 4,534 votes against 1,515; in the four precincts of our study the vote stood at 1,380 to 509 in favor of the Democrat. But in 1960 Brooke took the ward with 6,067 votes against 2,425 for his Democratic opponent, and the four precincts with 2,295 against 605—a dramatic reversal which not only boded well

---

[4]In Edward C. Banfield and Martha Derthick, eds., *A Report on Politics in Boston* (Cambridge, Mass.: Joint Center for Urban Studies of the Massachusetts Institute of Technology and Harvard University, 1960), chapter VI, pp. 45-81.

[5]David Danzig, "Bigotry and the Presidency," [American Jewish] *Committee Reporter,* May 1960, p. 21.

for Brooke's future,[6] but also strongly suggests that he did much
to win Negro votes for other Republican candidates.[7]

---

[6] In 1962 he was elected Attorney General, becoming the first Negro to
hold elective state office in Massachusetts history.

[7] Boston is not the only place where Kennedy did poorly among Negroes.
He also fared badly in the only two counties in Tennessee (Fayette and
Haywood) in which Negroes are a majority. Fayette has long been in-
auspicious ground for the major parties. In 1948 they got fewer than 300
votes there, the rest presumably going to Thurmond; in 1956, out of 1,968
votes, the Democrats received 639 (32.5 per cent) and the Republicans
a mere 358 (18.2 per cent). In 1960, however, the Republicans picked
up 1,370 votes, 48.9 per cent of the 2,799 cast. Haywood County went
to Kennedy, but with only 61 per cent of the major-party vote; in 1956
Stevenson had won 81.1 per cent of the major-party vote and 73.2 per
cent of the total cast. It had been expected that Tennessee Negroes would
favor Kennedy and perhaps give him the edge in the state (New York
Times, November 6, 1960). But in Fayette and Haywood counties special
efforts had been made to register Negro voters; Eisenhower's Department
of Justice had gone to court on their behalf, with the result that 700
Negroes were newly enrolled in Fayette alone (ibid., April 26, May 10
and 18, June 19, August 6, 1960). Negroes in those counties thus had
every reason to credit the Republican party with their improved political
condition.

2. BUFFALO

BUFFALO* is an industrial city, railroad center and lake port, with a population of 530,000. Its industries are diversified—autos and aircraft, flour milling, meat packing, iron and steel—but there its variety ends. A sociologist has described Buffalo as "an urban area of unusual uniformity":

> It does not show the great variations of wealth and poverty so typical of large cities throughout the world. It is solidly industrial and apparently provides for its people at a moderate minimum level at least. As it has often been described, it is a branch plant town. It is an area in which many of the great factories are quite typically led by men who are branch managers of an even larger corporation. It does not have the abundance of wealth and high level executives of a major home-office type of industrial city. It is not the home of large numbers of great captains of industry nor the home office of great companies. . . .[1]

Most of the labor force are skilled and unskilled workers. Buffalo is one of the most strongly unionized cities in America.

Uniformity extends also to religion. Nearly two-thirds of Buffalo's residents are Catholics.[2] All but six of its 27 wards have a Catholic majority; of these six, three are inhabited predominantly by Negroes.

Poles are the largest ethnic group in Buffalo—about 170,000, or 35 per cent of the population. Next in size is the German group, about 120,000, almost evenly divided between Catholics and Lutherans. There are about 100,000 Irish and about 85,000 Italians. Negroes—more than 70,000—are 13 per cent of the population. Other minorities include the Protestant Anglo-Americans and 26,000 Jews. The Germans, Irish, Anglo-Americans and Jews have been moving out of the city into middle- and high-income

*For information and help we are grateful to Victor Einach, regional director of the New York State Commission Against Discrimination; Robert A. Hoffman, executive director of the Board of Community Relations; Joseph Kaszubowski, attorney, and Ignacy Morawski of New York, editor of the Polish-language daily, *Nowy Swiat.*

[1] Thomas P. Imse, *Metropolitan Buffalo Perspectives: A Pilot Study Report for a Buffalo Metropolitan Area Survey* (Buffalo: Buffalo Redevelopment Foundation, October 1958), p. 38.

[2] Catholic diocesan census, September 1958, published in the Buffalo *Courier-Express,* November 14, 1958.

suburbs; the Poles, Italians and Negroes, for the most part, live in the central city and have low incomes.

German Lutherans were among the earliest settlers in Buffalo and many generations ago took a place of leadership in the Republican party. In contrast, the Poles, who came later to work on the railroads and in steel mills, grain elevators and meat packing plants, turned to the Democratic party, traditionally associated with the Irish and friendly to the New Immigration. One Polish informant we consulted said that the Poles became Democrats under the influence of the Irish clergy, who tried to Americanize them through the local political machine. Between the German-Lutheran-Republican and the Polish-Catholic-Democratic alignments, old-country religious, cultural and political conflicts continued. Animosities apparently persist even now in social and professional relations; it is said that a Polish doctor or lawyer cannot hope to develop a substantial clientele among Germans.

Ethnic conflicts have kept erupting within the Democratic party as well, though the Irish, the oldest, most acculturated and politically most experienced group, have retained control of the party machinery. Local patronage frequently has been dispensed along ethnic lines, and a detailed study of council elections and mayoral appointments would yield some understanding of the ethnic side of Buffalo politics.

The city's vote in the 1960 presidential election was not affected to any significant degree by local ethnic conflicts.[3] For Polish voters in particular, no ethnic factor was involved in the choice of candidates. Kennedy was championed by a relative descended from one of Poland's most illustrious families: his wife's brother-in-law, Prince Stanislas Radziwill. Nixon appealed to what he thought was the Polish interest by promising before an audience in Buffalo's Polish Union Hall on October 17, 1960, that, if elected, he would support Polish claims to formerly German lands by recognizing the Oder-Neisse line as Poland's western

---

[3]Cf. Louis Harris, "Some Observations on Election Behavior Research," *Public Opinion Quarterly*, XX (1956), 382, on a finding about New York City elections: " . . . class and nationality lines appear to polarize more in New York City in municipal elections than in either state-wide or even in national Presidential elections."

frontier. But this did not win Nixon any Polish votes; it only angered Germany.[4]

All observers interviewed agreed that among Poles of the low-income bracket economic issues count for more than ethnic ties. As one Polish resident put it, "belly means more than fatherland." Kennedy had strong labor-union support and was running during an economic recession. That, presumably, was his main appeal for Polish voters, though his Catholicism and Radziwill's support may have been contributing factors.

A Buffalo worker, so the story goes, was asked: "Are you going to vote for Kennedy because he is a Catholic?" He replied: "No, because I am." The remark is more than a joke. Despite the growth of a Catholic middle class, to be a Catholic in one of the great northern manufacturing cities and particularly in Buffalo today usually means to be an industrial worker with a fairly low income, and a Democrat.[5]

In the main, Buffalo has been rather strongly Democratic, though the city gave Eisenhower 50.4 per cent of its vote in 1952 and 57.7 per cent in 1956. Four years later Buffalo returned to the Democratic column, casting 65.0 per cent of its vote for Kennedy. Table 3 attempts to gauge the intensity of this return; it measures the figures for 1960 against a norm derived from the votes for U. S. Senator over a period of years, rather than from the untypical Eisenhower elections. The data show that in the city as a whole the vote in 1956 deviated more sharply from normal than in 1960: in 1956 the Democratic percentage dropped 12.4 points below normal, while in 1960 it rose 10.3 points above normal.

Was this emphatic return to the Democratic party a result of the religious issue—a response to Kennedy as a fellow Catholic? Was it motivated by unemployment, recession or the threat of

---

[4]In response to outcries in West Germany, the State Department had to issue a statement denying any change in America's attitude toward the Oder-Neisse line (New York *Times,* October 25, 1960).

[5]Cf. Donald J. Bogue, *The Population of the United States* (Glencoe, Ill., 1959), pp. 700, 703: "The outstanding fact . . . is that Roman Catholics comprise a disproportionately large share of the population in the most heavily industrialized areas" and "have an excess of urban working-class persons."

TABLE 3

DEMOCRATIC VOTE AND DEVIATIONS FROM THE
DEMOCRATIC NORM IN PRESIDENTIAL ELECTIONS
IN BUFFALO, 1952-1960

(Per Cent)

Area	Democratic norm*	Democratic vote and deviation		
		1952	1956	1960
Total city 63 per cent Catholic	54.7	49.6 (−5.1)	42.3 (−12.4)	65.0 (+10.3)
One low-income ward Negro	65.2	75.3 (+10.1)	58.9 (−6.3)	77.4 (+12.2)
Four low-income wards 75 per cent Polish, 90 per cent Catholic	71.0	67.8 (−3.2)	56.2 (−14.8)	78.6 (+7.6)
One upper-middle-income ward White, 54 per cent Catholic	39.5	34.0 (−5.5)	29.5 (−10.0)	44.7 (+5.2)
One middle-income ward White, 43 per cent Catholic	35.3	26.2 (−9.1)	26.5 (−8.8)	48.4 (+13.1)

* Computed from votes for U.S. Senator in 1950, 1956 and 1958, which were remarkably consistent. (The 1952 senatorial election was excluded because throughout the state the candidate failed to attract the usual Democratic vote.)

Source: Computed from data in Governmental Affairs Institute, *America Votes* (New York and Pittsburgh: Macmillan and University of Pittsburgh Press), vols. 1-3, 1956, 1958, 1959; Buffalo *Courier-Express*, Nov. 9, 1960.

automation and plant closings? Was it the work of a revitalized Democratic party organization in upstate New York? Or was it brought about by disappointment with Republican economic and labor policies? Labor leaders believe that Nixon's role in settling the steel strike early in 1960 boomeranged; many steelworkers were dissatisfied with the settlement, and David J. McDonald, president of the United Steelworkers of America, is said to have been booed in Buffalo while reporting on the positive aspects of the pact, particularly while praising Nixon's mediation. But no categorical explanation is possible, because the religious, economic and political factors cannot be isolated.

Table 3 further analyzes the voting of four different segments of the Buffalo population of diverse ethnic background, color, class and religion, which gave Kennedy more than a normal Democratic vote. A study of the fluctuations and differences among them, however small, may point up the factors decisive in each.

(1) A low-income ward inhabited by Negroes went massively for Kennedy. Buffalo's Negroes generally vote Democratic; they supported Stevenson overwhelmingly in 1952 and gave him a substantial majority in 1956. But the ward's vote for Kennedy, 77.4 per cent, was a full 12.2 percentage points above the Democratic norm for the area and 2.1 points above that for Stevenson in 1952. Compared with 1956, it represents a shift of 18.5 per cent away from the Republicans. As Protestants, the Negro voters obviously could not have been favorably influenced by the religious issue. Economic factors were almost certainly paramount. Perhaps Kennedy's dramatic telephone call to help release the Negro leader, Martin Luther King, from arrest in De Kalb County, Georgia, further confirmed Negro voters in their Democratic preference.

(2) Four low-income wards in East Buffalo, presumed to be about 75 per cent Polish and described as 90 per cent Catholic in the diocesan census, have been the city's most solidly Democratic wards, with a joint norm of 71 per cent. In 1956, though many Poles in these wards voted for Eisenhower, Stevenson maintained a comfortable majority of 56.2 per cent. But Nixon could not hold Eisenhower's small gains; in 1960 the wards actually exceeded their high Democratic norm by 7.6 per cent, giving Kennedy 78.6 per cent of their vote.

This margin of 7.6 per cent may reflect the particular appeal of a Catholic candidate, or it may mirror, at least in part, the hopes and expectations of low-income workers during a time of economic hardship. Most likely both economic and religious reasons favored the Democratic party. The economic factor is pointed up by Gallup poll findings, released December 10, 1960, that the Democrats won 65 per cent of union members' votes in the nation (compared with 57 per cent in 1956), 68 per cent in the East, and 70 per cent in cities of 500,000 or more. But these figures are not conclusive, because the Catholic and union groups overlap. Catholics predominate in organized labor, particularly in the East and in the largest cities; and 85 per cent of Catholic union members, as against only 52 per cent of Protestant, voted

Democratic. Thus there is no way of determining whether union-ism or Catholicism was the weightier factor.[6]

(3) A traditionally Republican upper-middle-income ward, one of the two highest-income wards in the city, gave Kennedy 44.7 per cent of its vote, or 5.2 per cent more than a Democratic candidate normally gets. Since there are no other apparent reasons for well-to-do Republicans to vote Democratic, this deviation might be ascribed to the religious issue. But the significance of the shift cannot be definitely assessed, because only 54 per cent of the ward's population is Catholic.

(4) A predominantly middle-class white ward, 43 per cent Catholic and traditionally Republican, gave 48.4 per cent of its votes to Kennedy and showed a pro-Kennedy deviation of 13.1 per cent, the highest in any ward studied. Among the area's sub-stantial Catholic population, consisting largely of professional peo-ple—some of them associated with the University of Buffalo, Canisius College and other institutions of learning—Kennedy's education and culture may have exerted some influence. But however the voters may have explained their choice to themselves, religion rather than class probably was the decisive reason for the unusual Democratic turnout in this normally Republican ward.

---

[6]A study by the Republican National Committee (*The 1960 Elections: A Summary Report with Supporting Tables,* Washington, April 1961, p. 14) uses the 1956 Eisenhower vote in various industrial centers as the base from which to measure the 1960 Catholic labor defection from the Repub-lican column, and consequently overestimates the effect of the religious issue on the union vote. Actually, among Catholic labor, the pro-Eisen-hower and anti-Stevenson factors in 1956 may well have been stronger than the pro-Kennedy factor in 1960. The study concludes that the Catholic issue cost Nixon votes in 1960; but Nixon could not reasonably be ex-pected to retain votes which in 1956 had gone to the Republicans only because of Eisenhower's personal popularity among Catholics or because of their marked dislike for Stevenson.

3. CINCINNATI

CINCINNATI,* an industrial center on the Ohio River with a population of just over 500,000, is one of the few large cities that traditionally have been and still are Republican. Germans have long been the dominant ethnic group. Starting about 1850, they arrived in such large numbers that the city became practically bilingual; until the First World War, German was taught in all public and parochial schools. Today the language is no longer widely spoken, but German influence in community affairs is said to remain pervasive.[1]

There are nearly 110,000 Negroes in Cincinnati—almost 22 per cent of the city's population. Tension between Negroes and whites is marked. One of the reasons may be found in the city's history: though Cincinnati was a station on the abolitionist Underground Railroad, it was also the center of Southern sympathizers in the North. Another cause may be the Southern race attitudes of the numerous mountaineers and backwoodsmen from Kentucky across the river, and from nearby Tennessee and West Virginia, who have been settling in the city. Finally, whites have seen a threat in the increasing political vigor of the Negro population. This fear was especially pronounced under Cincinnati's former system of proportional representation, and was the main reason for the staggering defeat of PR in 1957, after 32 years of operation.[2]

Catholics are an estimated 35 to 38 per cent of the population. Among them most of the Irish are Democrats, as are a minority of Italians and Germans. The Democratic party has often been called the Catholic party, and after the 1957 municipal election

---

*For information and advice we thank Marshall Bragdon, executive director of the Mayor's Friendly Relations Committee, and Professor Ralph A. Straetz of New York University.

[1]Kenneth E. Gray, *A Report on Politics in Cincinnati* (Cambridge, Mass.: Joint Center for Urban Studies of the Massachusetts Institute of Technology and Harvard University, 1959), chapter I, p. 5.

[2]Cf. Ralph A. Straetz, *PR Politics in Cincinnati: Thirty-two Years of City Government through Proportional Representation* (New York: New York University Press, 1958). The book includes a detailed study on the behavior of religious and racial groups in PR voting. See also Gray, *op. cit.,* chapter II, pp. 10f., 17-19.

Catholics were accused of voting as a bloc to elect candidates of their faith.[3]

Cincinnati voters have shown a conservative and isolationist tendency, which has expressed itself most specifically in opposition to foreign aid. Republican ex-Senators George H. Bender and John W. Bricker were the political exponents of this point of view. The tendency undoubtedly derives from the German background of many voters; the city's Germans have been largely isolationist since the First World War and even more so since the Second.

The vagaries of Cincinnati voting between 1952 and 1960 are evident in Table 4, which shows the Democratic percentage in the city as a whole, in a low-income Negro ward, in a predominantly Catholic, ethnically mixed working-class ward with lower-middle incomes, and in a predominantly German Catholic upper-middle-income ward. The city-wide Democratic percentage was unusually high in four instances: for Frank J. Lausche in the gubernatorial elections of 1954 (line 4) and 1956 (line 6), for Michael V. DiSalle in that of 1958 (line 9) and for Kennedy in 1960 (line 11). Its lowest ebb was in the 1956 presidential election (line 5). The same fluctuations may be observed even more clearly in the two Catholic wards. The Negro ward, on the other hand, departs from the pattern; here the vote has been preponderantly Democratic throughout, most likely for economic reasons, but perhaps also in opposition to the white Republican majority.

The returns suggest that Cincinnati has a fairly constant Democratic vote, as in lines 2, 3, 7, and 10. For the city as a whole, the senatorial election of 1954 comes closest to being a norm. In special circumstances the Democratic vote may be increased to a specific maximum. Kennedy's success in winning this extra vote, particularly in the Catholic wards, establishes with reasonable certainty that some voters were attracted by his religion. In this respect the large Democratic turnout for Kennedy differs from those for Lausche in 1956 and earlier, and from that for DiSalle in 1958. For even though these candidates, too, were Catholics, their faith apparently was not at issue nor its supposed effect on their fitness for high office. All over the United States Catholics

---

[3]Gray, *op. cit.,* chapter I, pp. 5f.; chapter II, pp. 30-32.

TABLE 4

DEMOCRATIC VOTE IN THREE WARDS
IN CINCINNATI, 1952-1960

(Per cent)

Election and candidate winning state	Total city	Negro, low-income ward	Catholic, ethnically mixed lower-middle income ward	German Catholic, upper-middle income ward
(1) President, 1952	43.2	81.2	49.0	37.1
(2) Senator, 1952 (Bricker, R.)	43.2	68.7	51.5	43.8
(3) Senator, 1954 (Bender, R.)	43.8	70.1	52.1	45.8
(4) *Governor, 1954 (Lausche, D.)	50.5	72.8	59.3	56.6
(5) President, 1956	37.5	72.2	42.0	30.5
(6) *Senator, 1956 (Lausche, D.)	51.3	73.7	57.7	54.9
(7) Governor, 1956 (O'Neill, R.)	44.0	70.5	53.4	44.2
(8) Senator, 1958 (Bricker, R.)	49.2	70.5	59.6	49.4
(9) *Governor, 1958 (DiSalle, D.)	54.6	74.5	67.1	57.6
(10) State Auditor, 1960 (Rhodes, R.)	46.4	79.6	56.0	48.5
(11) *President, 1960	50.4	83.8	60.3	56.5

* Democratic vote substantially above normal.

Source: Computed from data in Governmental Affairs Institute, *op. cit.*, and official returns for 1960 published by the Board of Elections of Cincinnati.

have long been accepted as senators and governors. The presidency, however, is different.

Lausche is in a sense a marginal Catholic, having been married outside the Church. His repeated successes almost certainly derive from his independent personality and the frugal conservatism of his administration. A son of Slovenian immigrants, he served five terms as Governor of Ohio, winning every election he entered except one, despite his being constantly at odds with the Democratic organization. He has usually run an independent campaign and seldom taken the stump for other Democratic candidates. On one occasion he said he had "a certain affinity" for Eisenhower; in the 1950 senatorial election he openly expressed admiration for Robert A. Taft and refused to back Taft's opponent, "Jumping Joe" Ferguson. This act is said to have earned him "the undying hatred of many party-first Democrats in Ohio";[4] on the other hand, he has enjoyed the constant and loyal support of normally Republican voters in Cincinnati and elsewhere.

As for DiSalle, his noteworthy 1958 victory must be viewed against his substantial defeats by the same voters in 1956 and in many earlier elections.[5] The 1958 Republican candidate was the incumbent, C. William O'Neill, a Baptist, whose administration had caused widespread disappointment and even talk of mismanagement. What sealed O'Neill's fate, though, was his devoted and enthusiastic support of a "right to work" law. He lost the state by 450,000 votes and the city by 16,000, while Senator Bricker, whose support for the proposed law had been half-hearted at best, was defeated for re-election by only 157,000 in the state and 2,500 in Cincinnati. The gubernatorial ballot would seem to have been in large measure a vote against O'Neill rather than a vote for DiSalle.

Fluctuations of the Democratic vote in the same wards and the city as a whole are measured in Table 5, with the 1954 senatorial returns serving as a norm (see page 24). As the data show, Kennedy's gains over the normal Democratic vote were comparable to Lausche's in 1954, except among Negroes. Among Cath-

---

[4]*Time*, February 20, 1956.
[5]He was defeated once again in 1962 by State Auditor James A. Rhodes.

TABLE 5

DEVIATIONS FROM THE DEMOCRATIC NORM IN FOUR
ELECTIONS IN CINCINNATI, 1952-1960

(Per cent)

Area	Democratic norm (Senatorial 1954)	Deviations from the Democratic norm			
		Stevenson 1952	Lausche 1954	Stevenson 1956	Kennedy 1960
Total city	43.8	− 0.6	+ 6.7	− 6.3	+ 6.6
Negro working-class (low-income) ward	70.1	+ 11.1	+ 2.7	+ 2.1	+ 13.7
Catholic working-class (lower-middle-income) ward	52.1	− 3.1	+ 7.2	− 10.1	+ 8.2
German Catholic middle-class (upper-middle-income) ward	45.8	− 8.7	+ 10.8	− 15.3	+ 10.7

Source: Computed from data in Governmental Affairs Institute, *op. cit.*, and official returns
for 1960 published by the Board of Elections of Cincinnati.

olics and in the city as a whole, Kennedy won back the normal
Democratic vote plus the support of those who vote Democratic
only on special occasions. But even more striking than Kennedy's
ability to win back the Democratic regulars was Stevenson's failure
to hold them in 1956. The largest drop below the Democratic
norm in 1956 occurred among Catholics, especially those of the
middle class—a deviation greater than their rise above the norm
four years later.

The data in Table 5, like those for Buffalo, suggest that
entirely apart from his national popularity Eisenhower was particularly attractive to Catholics or, possibly, that Stevenson was
especially repugnant to them. If so, then Kennedy's religion was
not the sole reason why urban working-class and middle-class
Catholics returned to the Democratic party in 1960. To some
degree the Democratic surge in 1960 may have been only apparent, a consequence of basing comparison on the untypical election
of 1956, when neither candidate had been a characteristic party
symbol or spokesman. Nevertheless, it still remains a matter for
speculation whether Nixon might have duplicated Eisenhower's

feat of gaining their support if his opponent had not been a Catholic.

The 1960 deviation from the normal Democratic vote, as shown in Table 5, does not differ as markedly between the Catholic working-class ward (+8.2) and the Catholic middle-class ward (+10.7) as it does between corresponding areas in Buffalo (+7.6 and +13.1). It seems reasonable to suggest that among the workers class interest combined with the religious factor to strengthen the shift to the Democratic candidate. In the middle-class ward, a normally Republican, predominantly German area, the class factor presumably was absent, and religion would appear to have been the main reason for Kennedy's success.[6]

---

[6]The impact of the religious issue upon German Catholics who have voted Republican for the last twenty years is even more conclusively illustrated in the case of Clinton County, a semi-rural region in downstate Illinois. About 75 per cent of the county's 24,000 people are Catholics, and most are of German origin. Heavily Democratic before the Second World War, Clinton turned Republican in 1940 and remained so until 1960, when it went for Kennedy. The Republican majorities had their origin in anti-interventionist and isolationist views, largely determined by German ethnic identification. The Democratic vote in 1960 may be ascribed to the religious issue, since ethnic factors no doubt would have kept the county Republican. County-wide presidential returns since 1928 follow:

Presidential Election	Democratic Percentage
1928	69.1
1932	75.2
1936	59.4
1940	37.5
1944	36.9
1948	48.2
1952	41.8
1956	36.5
1960	51.8

4. PROVIDENCE

PROVIDENCE,* an economically stagnant community during recent years, is of mixed ethnic character. In 1954 the Rhode Island Board of Elections, checking the names on registration rolls throughout the state, concluded that 27 per cent of the city's people had Italian names, 26 per cent Irish, and 21 per cent English or Scottish. Since there has been little population movement, this survey still gives an accurate picture.[1]

Italians were found sufficiently grouped together to form overwhelming majorities in as many as five of the ward districts into which the city is divided for purposes of municipal government. No other group was so concentrated; but particularly large numbers of English and Scottish names are found in three State Representative districts—those where incomes are highest.[2]

In addition to these major groups the Board of Elections survey found smaller numbers of Armenian, French, German, Jewish, Polish and Portuguese names in the city. For the most part, these groups are scattered; no one of them can be said to predominate in any of the city's political units, except that in two ward districts there is a large concentration of Portuguese names. The bearers of these are Negroes from the Cape Verde Islands, a Portuguese possession in the Atlantic Ocean.

Providence is a Democratic city—not surprisingly perhaps, in view of the fact that Irish and Italians constitute 53 per cent of its population. Stevenson polled more than 57 per cent of the local vote in 1952, and even in 1956 he won a majority though a slim one. In 1960 the Democratic party carried the city overwhelmingly; Kennedy received more than 72 per cent of the vote,

---

*We are indebted to Professor Elmer E. Cornwell of Brown University for his help, his knowledge and his time.

[1] The only exceptions—two ward districts where urban renewal has displaced Negro residents—do not affect the present study.

[2] All socio-economic data are from Sidney Goldstein and Kurt B. Mayer, *The Ecology of Providence: Basic Social and Demographic Data by Census Tracts* (Providence, R. I.: Brown University, 1958). The authors note that population estimates by census tracts were made in 1956 by the Bureau of the Census, and some of their computations are based on 1956 data.

and Claiborne de B. Pell, running for the Senate, more than 76 per cent. The Democratic candidate for Governor, John A. Notte, Jr., got 62.5 per cent of the city's ballots, enough to elect him comfortably.

The five overwhelmingly Italian ward districts mentioned earlier are Nos. 4/2 (i.e., District 2 of Ward 4), 4/4, 7/4, 13/3 and 13/5. The percentage of Italians in all five taken together is about 87.5; in 4/4 it is more than 80, and in 13/3 more than 92.5. Foreign-born persons make up 20 to 25 per cent of the population in 4/2, 13/3 and 13/5, and 15 to 20 per cent in the other two. In 4/2 and 7/4, 10 to 15 percent are without schooling;[3] in the others, 5 to 10 per cent. The residents are overwhelmingly blue-collar workers, and very few—under 1 per cent in 4/2 and 1 to 3 per cent in the others—have family incomes in excess of $10,000.

Since the Italian districts are similar to one another, we may compute their vote as a unit in making comparisons with the total city vote. True, over the years each ward district has shown a distinctive degree of attachment to the Democratic party, but the differences are not great. Democratic loyalty is high in all five, and defections occur only when a Republican candidate who is an Italian runs against a Democrat who is not.[4]

As Table 6 shows, the five Italian ward districts cast 78.5 per cent of their vote for Kennedy and 80.5 per cent for Pell, exceeding the city-wide percentages by 6 and 4 points respectively. Contrary to what might have been expected, the vote for Kennedy does not seem to have been cut down by rivalry between Italians and Irish.[5] Thus we may wonder what neutralized this traditional dislike and made Kennedy so popular among Italians. In inter-

---

[3]Ten to fifteen per cent is the highest illiteracy category in the study by Goldstein and Mayer.

[4]According to Duane Lockard, *New England State Politics* (Princeton, N.J.: Princeton University Press, 1959), p. 200, not any Italian will have this effect, but only one who can serve as a "symbol of success."

[5]Cf., for example, the following remark by Elmer E. Cornwell: "Almost as frequently noted as the prominence of the Irish politician, has been the growing rivalry posed for him by the numerous and more recently arrived Italians" ("Party Absorption of Ethnic Groups: The Case of Providence, Rhode Island," *Social Forces*, XXXVIII [1959-60], 206).

TABLE 6

DEMOCRATIC VOTE IN FIVE PREDOMINANTLY ITALIAN WARD DISTRICTS IN PROVIDENCE, 1952-1960

(Per cent)

Election	Total city	Five Italian ward districts
1952: Senator Pastore (D) vs. Ewing (R)	64.5	78.7
1952: Governor Roberts (D) vs. Archambault (R)	61.3	73.0
1954: Governor Roberts (D) vs. Lewis (R)	65.8	73.8
1956: Governor Roberts (D) vs. Del Sesto (R)	54.6	48.8
1958: Senator Pastore (D) vs. Ewing (R)	72.9	77.5
1958: Governor Roberts (D) vs. Del Sesto (R)	55.4	48.8
1960: President Kennedy (D) vs. Nixon (R)	72.2	78.5
1960: Senator Pell (D) vs. Archambault (R)	76.1	80.5
1960: Governor Notte (D) vs. Del Sesto (R)	62.5	65.9

Source: Computed from Rhode Island Board of Elections, *Official Count of the Ballots Cast*, 1952, 1954, 1956, 1958, 1960.

preting the same phenomenon among Boston voters, we noted that Italians still are in a relatively early stage of winning their way in American life, and suggested that they might therefore have been especially sensitive to the religious issue, recognizing anti-Catholicism as a possible check on their ambitions. It may well be that the same consideration obtains in Providence.

The solid Italian vote for Pell, an upper-class Episcopalian Yankee, may seem surprising, yet actually he had strong support among virtually all of the ethnic and religious groups in Rhode Island. In the 1960 primary he unexpectedly scored a thorough victory over Dennis J. Roberts and J. Howard McGrath—both former Governors and both representative of the state's Democratic "establishment." In the election itself, he was opposed by

Raoul Archambault, Jr., a French Canadian of great prominence in the Republican party[6] and its candidate for Governor in 1952; yet he carried the state with ease, actually winning more than 78 per cent of the vote in Woonsocket, where about 65 per cent of the population is French Canadian. Rhode Island politics being what it is, one may suspect that Pell's popularity derives in no small degree from his being a newcomer.

Support for major Democratic candidates is normally several percentage points higher in the five Italian ward districts than in Providence as a whole. But what happens when an Italian is a candidate is illustrated by the vote for Christopher Del Sesto, Republican, in the 1956 and 1958 gubernatorial contests. As the figures in Table 6 show, Del Sesto's candidacy occasioned a marked crossing of party lines in the five districts. The crossing over would be even more apparent if it were possible to eliminate Italian votes from the comparative figures for Providence as a whole; the city-wide Democratic percentages would then appear higher in the Del Sesto elections and lower in the rest, sharpening the contrast between Italians and others in both cases.

Del Sesto's opponent, Roberts, had comfortably carried the city in earlier contests: against Archambault in 1952 and against Dean J. Lewis in 1954. In the five Italian ward districts he had done exceptionally well. When he ran against Del Sesto in 1956, his city-wide percentage—including the votes of Italians—declined, and in the five districts, taken as a unit, he actually lost.[7] He carried the state by little more than 700 votes and there were charges of fraud, which inspired some sympathy for Del Sesto. Two years later Del Sesto defeated Roberts by about 6,000 votes. But the added support does not seem to have come from Providence; the change in Del Sesto's favor was less than one per cent

---

[6] The importance of French Canadians in Rhode Island is illustrated by the fact that they have long held one of the state's two seats in the U. S. House of Representatives. The incumbent is Fernand J. St. Germain, a Democrat; he was preceded by Aimé J. Forand. At the polls Forand was often opposed by Republicans of French Canadian ancestry; so was St. Germain.

[7] He did get 51.7 per cent of the vote in District 7/4, and 55 per cent in District 13/5, the most Democratic of the five. But in 1954 these two had given him 75 per cent and 80 per cent respectively. In 1952 he had done even better, with 78 per cent in 7/4 and 80.8 per cent in 13/5.

in the city, and in the Italian ward districts it was hardly notice-able. Evidently the Italian voters had already given him their full support in 1956.

Clearly, then, for the Italian voters of Providence an Italian name is a major attraction. This conclusion is confirmed by the senatorial returns in 1958, when the Democratic incumbent, John O. Pastore, opposed by Republican Bayard Ewing, ran about 30 per cent ahead of Roberts, his gubernatorial running mate, in the Italian districts.

Catholic Negroes from the Portuguese Cape Verde Islands predominate in Ward District 1/3 and 1/4; more than 60 per cent of the voters here have Portuguese names. The two districts are part of an area where in 1950 between 15 and 20 per cent of the population was foreign-born, 10 to 15 per cent completely lacked schooling, 70 to 80 per cent of employed residents were blue-collar workers, and 20 to 25 per cent of families and indi-viduals living alone earned less than $500 per year.[8] In recent elections the two Portuguese ward districts have voted overwhelm-ingly Democratic. In 1960 they gave almost 85 per cent of their vote to Kennedy, more than 86 per cent to Pell and more than 76 per cent to Notte—all well above the city-wide percentages. In 1958 they cast over 82 per cent of their vote for Pastore and over 74 per cent for Roberts, topping the city averages by about 10 and 19 per cent, respectively. And in 1956 Stevenson polled 62.7 per cent here, though he barely squeezed through in Providence as a whole. Thus the Portuguese districts show the strong Democratic preference usually found in working-class neighborhoods; whatever influence the Negro and Catholic character of the area may have exerted on the 1960 voting is concealed by the economic factor.

Though Kennedy did extraordinarily well in Providence, the race was very close in the three State Representative districts[9]

---

[8]Goldstein and Mayer, *op. cit.*

[9]These are districts for the election of representatives to the state legislature. They are used here because in the smaller ward districts English and Scottish names do not occur in sufficient numbers to permit analysis. The data from the name survey, originally reported by ward districts, have been regrouped accordingly. Conversely, in our analyses of the Italian and Cape Verde Negro votes, election returns by State Representative districts have been translated into ward-district figures.

where the concentration of English and Scottish names is greatest
(Table 7). All three are located in the city's most prosperous
areas; Goldstein and Mayer report that in the 3rd District more
than 20 per cent of families earned over $10,000 per year, the
highest income category of their study.

TABLE 7

MAJOR ETHNIC GROUPS IN THREE UPPER-INCOME
STATE REPRESENTATIVE DISTRICTS IN PROVIDENCE, 1954*

(Per cent)

District	English and Scottish names	Irish names	Jewish names
2	1,580	1,463	525
3	1,566	1,318	1,431
4	2,295	1,659	775

* Figures for smaller groups not shown.
Source: Rhode Island Board of Elections, *Survey of Rhode Island Electors*, 1954.

TABLE 8

DEMOCRATIC AND REPUBLICAN VOTE IN THREE UPPER-
INCOME STATE REPRESENTATIVE DISTRICTS WITH GREATEST
YANKEE CONCENTRATION IN PROVIDENCE, 1960

(Per cent)

Party	Office		
	President	Senator	Governor
Democratic	Kennedy 51.3 (Catholic)	Pell 59.3 (Yankee Protestant)	Notte 41.3 (Italian Catholic)
Republican	Nixon 48.7 (Protestant)	Archambault 40.7 (French-Canadian Catholic)	Del Sesto 58.7 (Italian Catholic)

Source: Computed from Rhode Island Board of Elections, *Official Count of the Ballots Cast*, 1960.

The three districts, taken together, went to Kennedy by only a little more than 51 per cent of the vote (Table 8); in the 2nd he lost, with 48.5 per cent. Since most of the area's Jewish and Irish residents were known to be strongly for Kennedy, most of the Yankees must have supported Nixon. In the gubernatorial contest, where two Italians were pitted against each other, the Republican won; Notte, the Democrat, received only 41 per cent of the three districts' combined vote, as against a city average of 62.5 per cent. But, interestingly, in the senatorial race the same districts gave more than 59 per cent of their vote to the Yankee Democrat Pell and less than 41 per cent to the French Canadian Republican Archambault.[10]

Thus the Yankee vote for the Democrat Pell in 1960 was not unlike the Italian vote for the Republican Del Sesto in 1958: a crossing of party lines to favor a fellow ethnic.[11]

---

[10] We were informed by a member of the Brown University faculty that many of these voters changed their registration from Republican to Democratic that year, presumably in order to vote for Pell in the primary against McGrath and Roberts. This became known when they tried to restore their Republican registration in time to vote in the 1962 primary, only to learn that the Rhode Island law required them to wait 26 months.

[11] Similar observations may be made about Yankees in Massachusetts—for example, in four middle- and upper-middle-income precincts of Boston's 5th Ward, inhabited mostly by persons of Yankee extraction. In the 1960 gubernatorial election, the Democratic candidate, Joseph D. Ward, an Irishman, received 26.0 per cent of the vote in these precincts, losing to John R. Volpe an Italian (see Table 2). In 1962 Governor Volpe ran for reelection against a Yankee Democrat, Endicott Peabody, 3rd; the vote for Peabody in the same precinct was 34.9 per cent, representing a Democratic increase of about one third. And Professor Murray B. Levin informs us that in the small towns of central and western Massachusetts, traditionally Republican and largely Yankee, Peabody won about 50,000 more votes than Democratic gubernatorial candidates usually do.

5. LOS ANGELES

IN CALIFORNIA as a whole Jews were the strongest Kennedy supporters among the three major religious groups (Table 9), according to the California Poll, a series of pre-election surveys released to the press.[1]

TABLE 9

PRESIDENTIAL PREFERENCES, BY RELIGION, IN CALIFORNIA, 1960

Religion	Number interviewed	Percentage		
		Kennedy	Nixon	Undecided
Protestants	730	38	56	6
Catholics	286	73	22	5
Jews	64	91	8	1

Source: Eugene C. Lee and William Buchanan, "The 1960 Election in California," *Western Political Quarterly*, XIV (1961), No. 1, Part II (Totton J. Anderson, ed., "The 1960 Elections in the West"), 319.

In Los Angeles County* a study of actual voting in 1960 also found Jews stanchly Democratic (81.7 per cent), but Spanish-speaking Mexicans and Negroes even more so (89.2 and 86.4 per cent, respectively).[2] The same study reported that in 1960 registered Democrats were 93.7 per cent of the electorate in 20 heavily Spanish-speaking Mexican precincts, 79.5 per cent in 75 heavily Negro precincts, and 80 per cent in 35 heavily Jewish precincts—as against 57.9 per cent in the county as a whole. The intense Democratic allegiance of the three groups is confirmed by the returns from one Jewish area and several Negro and Mexican ones within the county.

---

*Erwin L. Feiertag, assistant director of the Los Angeles office of the American Jewish Committee, provided useful information.

[1] Eugene C. Lee and William Buchanan, "The 1960 Election in California," *Western Political Quarterly*, XIV (1961), No. 1, Part II (Totton J. Anderson, ed., "The 1960 Elections in the West"), 318f.

[2] James Bassett, "Ethnic Groups Remain Solidly Democratic," Los Angeles *Times*, May 26, 1961.

The Jewish neighborhood studied consists of seven precincts in the Beverly-Fairfax district.[3] Approximately 70 per cent of the residents are Jews, most of whom have lived in Los Angeles for ten years or more. Over 60 per cent of them are native-born; roughly a third speak Yiddish, and of the foreign-born minority most are from Eastern Europe. About half of the heads of households are proprietors, managers or professionals, over 30 per cent are salesmen or other white-collar employees, and the rest are workers. In 1951 the median income in the neighborhood was $5,370, the same as for Jews in the city as a whole. In the same year, about 30 per cent had had at least some college training and another 35 per cent had had a high-school education. About 35 per cent thought anti-Semitism was a very serious problem.[4]

In 1960 Kennedy swept the area, winning 95 per cent of the vote. Nixon received only 67 of the 1,399 ballots cast for the two major parties; four years earlier Eisenhower had polled 105 votes (7.3 per cent) in the same precincts. In seeking to explain why these voters supported Kennedy in 1960 even more strongly than they had Stevenson in 1956, we can hardly conclude that they actually were more attracted to Kennedy; it seems, rather, that they were repelled by Nixon, in more ways than one. Not only did they share the liberals' persistent mistrust of him; many also believed the rumor that he was anti-Semitic. It was among the middle-class Jews of Los Angeles that these rumors first began to spread, and prompt denials by non-partisan Jewish organizations apparently had little influence on them.

Two heavily Negro assembly districts and one Mexican district voted Democratic, giving Kennedy more votes than they had cast for Stevenson in 1952. The figures (Table 10) suggest that Kennedy won back many of the votes that had gone to Eisenhower; the Mexicans' return to the Democratic fold was less marked, because their switch to Eisenhower had been on a smaller scale.

---

[3]The precincts were Nos. 1654, 1656, 1657, 1659, 1661, 1662, 1665.

[4]Fred Massarik, *A Report on the Jewish Population of Los Angeles* (Los Angeles: Jewish Community Council, 1953); *idem, A Report on the Jewish Population of Los Angeles: 1959* (Los Angeles: Jewish Federation-Council, 1959). The 1959 report did not contain data on income.

TABLE 10

DEMOCRATIC VOTE IN NEGRO AND MEXICAN DISTRICTS
IN LOS ANGELES, 1952-1960

(Per cent)

Assembly District	Ethnic character	Election			
		Presidential 1952	Presidential 1956	Gubernatorial 1958	Presidential 1960
55	Negro	72.8	68.8	82.9	77.6
62	Negro	77.4	72.0	81.7	82.1
40	Mexican	71.0	71.3	80.4	75.4

Source: Computed from data in Governmental Affairs Institute, *op. cit.*, and official returns for 1960 published by the Registrar of Voters of the County of Los Angeles.

Except in one of the Negro districts, the vote for Kennedy was lower than that for Edmund S. Brown, the Democratic candidate for Governor in 1958. This finding might suggest that some Negroes and Mexicans, like many whites, had been attracted to Eisenhower as an individual rather than a Republican, that they were now returning to the Democratic party as a party, and that Kennedy was no more popular with them than other Democratic candidates. But the 1958 vote for Brown is no measure of normal Democratic allegiance. It was unusually high because within the Republican party there was resentment over the way in which ex-Senator William F. Knowland had displaced former Governor Goodwin J. Knight as the gubernatorial candidate. In addition, Knowland's support of a "right to work" law, then on the ballot throughout the state, undoubtedly lost him votes in working-class districts such as these.

The Religious Issue in Rural Areas

6. FUNDAMENTALISTS:
TENNESSEE, ILLINOIS, OHIO

THE virulence of anti-Catholic propaganda during the election campaign and the history of anti-Catholicism among Protestants, particularly Fundamentalists, dictated that we examine some places where the influence of anti-Catholic Fundamentalism on the election might be seen. For this purpose we selected counties in Tennessee, southern Illinois and southern Ohio.

Tennessee

Tennessee* differs from other Southern states in the kind of men it sends to the United States Senate. Estes Kefauver is unquestionably a liberal, and Albert Gore is moderate to liberal. Both have gained nationwide reputations through their serious interest in national problems, and both refused to sign the "Southern Manifesto" of March 1956, in which Southern Senators and Congressmen pledged themselves to seek a reversal of the 1954 Supreme Court decision outlawing racial segregation in public schools. In his 1960 campaign for a third-term nomination, Kefauver was opposed by a conservative who was vocal in his support of segregation; Kefauver's chances were regarded as poor, but he won handsomely, receiving about 65 per cent of the vote.

All this suggests that the issue of liberalism vs. conservatism, and even that of states' rights vs. Federal power, so often crucial in Southern elections, had little effect on the 1960 voting in Tennessee. Yet despite this fact, and despite traditional adherence to the Democratic party, Tennessee went to Nixon. Eisenhower had polled 50.1 per cent of the statewide vote for the two major parties in 1952 and 50.3 per cent in 1956. Since much of his success everywhere had been due to his personal popularity, many of his supporters, especially in the South, were expected to return to the Democratic party in 1960. Instead, Nixon won 53.6 per cent of Tennessee's major-party vote.

In large part this outcome may be explained by the impact of Kennedy's Catholicism—a major campaign issue in the state—

---

*We are grateful to Professor William Goodman of the University of Tennessee for the information he provided.

41

upon predominantly Protestant and Fundamentalist voters. Over 95 per cent of reported church members in Tennessee are Protestants and fewer than 3.5 per cent are Roman Catholics. Of the Protestants more than 52 per cent belong to the Southern Baptist Convention, a Fundamentalist denomination, whose then president, the Rev. Ramsay Pollard, played a leading role in the anti-Catholic phase of the campaign. Second in size are the Methodists, who make up more than 28 per cent of the Protestant total. The Methodist church cannot be definitely characterized as Fundamentalist or non-Fundamentalist, because it embraces several formerly separate denominations and traditionally allows doctrinal freedom; nevertheless, many of its members are believed to have been susceptible to the religious issue.

Table 11 presents the Democratic share of the major-party presidential vote since 1944 in eleven counties. All eleven are overwhelmingly Protestant, with Baptists and Methodists predominating; even Shelby County, which includes the city of Memphis and has relatively large numbers of Catholics and Jews, is mainly Fundamentalist.

In 1960 the eleven counties turned Republican. In each of them the Democratic share of the major party vote fell conspicuously below what it had been even in 1948—the year the States' Rights candidate, Strom Thurmond, won 13.4 per cent of the Tennessee vote, mostly at Harry S. Truman's expense. Two counties, Dyer and Madison, appeared in the Republican column for the first time since 1872. Except in the Eisenhower elections, not one of the eleven had gone Republican since 1928. Even in 1928, only three did so, which would seem to suggest that in Tennessee, contrary to what is supposed to be the national trend, the religious issue has become more, not less, important since Al Smith ran.

Downstate Illinois

The southern tip of Illinois is in part a mining region, in part hilly, scrubby fruit-growing and farm country. Its economy is depressed and its population declining. The Southern Baptist Convention is the area's dominant religious body, with an influence that extends beyond the enrolled membership.

TABLE 11

DEMOCRATIC SHARE OF MAJOR-PARTY VOTE FOR PRESIDENT IN ELEVEN TENNESSEE COUNTIES, 1944-1960

(Per cent)

County	1944	1948	1952	1956	1960	Previous Republican victories (since 1872)
Chester	55.4	56.1	47.0	50.6	39.7	1952
Clay	53.7	62.0	53.5	51.2	47.1	1920
Crockett	64.5	70.2	61.6	65.7	49.3	1920
Decatur	55.1	54.8	54.5	50.7	44.0	1904, 1908, 1916, 1920
Dyer	73.9	71.7	58.4	62.8	48.6	None
Fayette	82.2	77.4*	53.3	64.1	39.4	1872, 1876, 1880, 1884
Lawrence	51.7	55.9	48.5	48.0	46.0	1904, 1908, 1916, 1920, 1924, 1928, 1952, 1956
Madison	76.1	73.7	54.3	56.3	39.6	None
Meigs	57.7	51.3	47.0	47.3	43.4	1916, 1920, 1924, 1928, 1952, 1956
Shelby	81.8	62.1	52.4	48.6	49.7	1880, 1884, 1956
Sullivan	54.1	52.2	43.2	42.2	39.2	1928, 1952, 1956

* The major parties got only 300 votes altogether.

Source: Computed from figures published in the *World Almanac* and Governmental Affairs Institute, *op. cit.* Information in last column provided by Professor William Goodman of the University of Tennessee.

Political analysts have observed that downstate Illinois was affected by the religious issue. This observation is confirmed by an analysis of voting in three of the region's counties—Franklin, Jefferson and Union—where most church members are affiliated with the Southern Baptist Convention and the number of Catholics is negligible. Franklin County is chiefly a mining district; Jefferson has mines, farming and some manufactures; Union is primarily agricultural.

For the last forty years the three counties have generally voted Democratic, though they gave more of their votes to Eisenhower than to previous Republican presidential candidates. In 1960, surprisingly, they did even better for Nixon—but not necessarily because they preferred him to Eisenhower or because the Democratic ties which Eisenhower had loosened were dissolved.

Table 12 reports the counties' presidential vote since 1928, as compared with that for Governor. Before 1960 the presidential returns corresponded roughly to the national ups and downs (except that Union gave somewhat more support to Stevenson in 1956 than in 1952). The gubernatorial vote for the most part paralleled the presidential. In the three counties as a whole, the only conspicuously big difference between the two occurred in 1956, probably because in that year a graft scandal involving the State Treasurer cut down the Republican vote for state offices; an earlier large difference (1932) was limited to Franklin County. In view of the region's political traditions and economic problems, one might have expected a return to the Democratic presidential column in 1960. But Kennedy did not make up the Democratic losses of 1952 and 1956 or close the gap between the presidential and gubernatorial voting. His support actually dropped a little below Stevenson's in 1956, and he trailed the Democratic candidate for Governor by 5 to 6 percentage points. In the absence of other reasons, Fundamentalist anti-Catholicism would seem to account for Kennedy's poor showing here.

As Table 12 shows, Kennedy fared worse than Al Smith in 1928. Smith did comparatively well in the three counties, polling a small majority in two and leading the gubernatorial candidate in the third. Perhaps the religious issue was less important in Smith's

TABLE 12

DEMOCRATIC VOTE FOR PRESIDENT AND GOVERNOR IN THREE DOWNSTATE ILLINOIS COUNTIES, 1928-1960

(Per cent)

Year	Franklin			Jefferson			Union		
	Presidential	Gubernatorial	Difference	Presidential	Gubernatorial	Difference	Presidential	Gubernatorial	Difference
1928	53.5	57.9	− 4.4	44.6	41.6	+3.0	55.3	56.8	− 1.5
1932	66.1	55.6	+10.5	64.0	61.3	+2.7	68.3	68.8	− 0.5
1936	58.8	56.0	+ 2.8	58.4	58.0	+0.4	60.0	59.3	+0.7
1940	54.5	52.6	+ 1.9	55.6	54.6	+1.0	54.1	54.9	− 0.8
1944	50.6	50.6	0.0	51.8	50.5	+1.3	51.5	51.9	− 0.4
1948	55.5	59.6	− 4.1	54.7	55.8	−1.1	53.7	56.3	− 2.6
1952	50.5	51.6	− 1.1	46.9	48.8	−1.9	48.0	50.3	− 2.3
1956	49.0	56.0	− 7.0	45.6	53.2	−7.6	50.9	58.9	− 8.0
1960	48.9	55.1	− 6.2	44.0	49.1	−5.1	49.5	54.6	− 5.1

Source: Computed from data in Samuel Kimball Gove, *Illinois Votes, 1900-1958* (Urbana, Ill.: University of Illinois, 1959); Chicago *Sun-Times,* November 10, 1960.

time. Or possibly there was less ticket-splitting; the electorate may have been less sophisticated then and less inclined to pick and choose. Also, in 1960 more people voted than in 1928, and it may be that this greater participation brought more Fundamentalists to the polls. Finally, it is possible that anti-Catholic propaganda was more widely distributed and proved more effective than in 1928.

In these downstate Illinois counties, as in the Tennessee counties discussed earlier, Kennedy's religion seems to be the only likely factor to account for his poor showing. Perhaps religion has become a kind of last-ditch issue with some Fundamentalists. Over the last four or five decades, they have reluctantly had to come to terms with many social and political innovations. A Catholic in the White House may well have seemed to them too stark a proof that the old America is disappearing.

Southern Ohio

The religious issue was a factor also in the southern tier of Ohio, where Methodists, Lutherans and various evangelicals predominate, and Catholics are almost unknown. Six counties were examined: Adams, Fayette, Gallia, Highland, Jackson and Pike—all, except Pike, Republican. The population is of German, Welsh, Scottish and English ancestry and has been settled there for many generations. Farming, tobacco culture, dairying and raising livestock are the major occupations, but small industrial centers in each county have diversified the economy; many farmers are also part-time workers. In Adams the population dropped a little between 1950 and 1960. In the others it increased slightly, but at less than the average growth rate of 9 per cent for rural Ohio reported in the 1960 census.

Table 13 shows the Democratic percentage of the presidential vote since 1928 in these counties. In all six Kennedy did better than Smith in 1928, but by the standards of the intervening elections the improvement was modest. He fell slightly below Roosevelt's showing of 1944 (a year when isolationism is believed to have cut down the Democratic vote) in four counties. In five counties he did not even come close to matching Truman's vote of 1948 and he barely topped Stevenson's 1956 performance, the Democratic low for the region since Smith.

TABLE 13

DEMOCRATIC VOTE FOR PRESIDENT
IN SIX SOUTHERN OHIO COUNTIES, 1928-1960

(Per cent)

Year	Adams	Fayette	Gallia	Highland	Jackson	Pike
1928	34.6	34.4	25.8	31.5	28.0	45.5
1932	54.9	54.8	42.6	50.6	44.4	65.1
1936	49.7	54.5	41.0	52.0	49.8	64.2
1940	44.8	46.7	35.1	44.8	45.8	61.0
1944	41.7	39.9	31.5	40.1	40.7	56.0
1948	45.7	41.9	37.4	45.3	46.7	63.1
1952	41.1	36.3	31.8	37.9	40.8	56.6
1956	40.9	34.0	29.0	36.5	35.3	52.8
1960	39.4	35.9	31.5	38.0	41.0	54.0

Source: Computed from election returns in the *World Almanac*, 1935-1957; Cleveland *Plain Dealer*, November 13, 1960.

Smith's poor showing compared with Kennedy's may well have been a consequence of the prohibition issue of 1928. Besides disapproving of Smith as a Catholic, the voters of the region—many of them members of the Methodist church, the leading advocate of prohibition—had presumably opposed him as the "wet" candidate. With liquor no longer an issue in national elections, though still of concern in the region,[1] Kennedy was less handicapped; but the religious factor may nevertheless have worked against him.

The religious issue may have been more significant than is apparent from the history of presidential voting alone. Table 14 compares the 1960 presidential vote of the six counties with the 1958 gubernatorial as well as the 1958 and 1956 senatorial returns, and shows that the proportion of votes for Kennedy is consistently smaller. The 1956 senatorial and 1958 gubernatorial votes set Democratic records in all of Ohio. Helped by personal

---

[1] In 1962 some townships in each of the six counties banned liquor under the state's local-option law. According to information obtained from the Licensed Beverage Industries, the percentage of people in "dry" areas ranged from 16.8 in Fayette County to 81.2 in Adams, as against a state average of 10.2.

TABLE 14

DEMOCRATIC VOTE FOR SENATOR, GOVERNOR AND PRESIDENT IN SIX SOUTHERN OHIO COUNTIES, 1956-1960

(Per cent)

County	1956 Senatorial (Lausche)	1958 Senatorial (Young)	1958 Gubernatorial (DiSalle)	1960 Presidential (Kennedy)
Adams	48.5	45.4	47.8	39.4
Fayette	50.4	37.4	42.3	35.9
Gallia	39.6	37.7	42.0	31.5
Highland	51.9	40.7	43.8	38.0
Jackson	46.1	48.1	53.3	41.0
Pike	60.8	62.1	64.4	54.0

Source: Computed from data in Governmental Affairs Institute, *op. cit.;* Cleveland *Plain Dealer,* November 13, 1960.

popularity and special issues—a proposed "right to work" law and doubts about the integrity of the state administration then in power—Lausche and DiSalle did as well as Truman in 1948 or better. By comparison, the Democratic senatorial candidate in 1958, Young, proved only moderately attractive. But Kennedy not only failed to attain Lausche's high, he even trailed Young.

In the absence of any more persuasive factor, we may be justified in concluding that some Protestants hesitated to vote Democratic because they did not want a Catholic as President. If religion had not been a factor, the six counties' vote for Kennedy probably would have been 2 to 6 percentage points higher.[2]

---

[2]Similar conclusions, some presented firmly and some tentatively, have been drawn for other states. Cf. Boyd A. Martin, "The 1960 Election in Idaho"; John M. Swarthout, "The 1960 Election in Oregon"; Hugh A. Bone, "The 1960 Election in Washington," in *Western Political Quarterly, loc. cit.*

7. FRENCH CATHOLICS, ANGLO-AMERICAN PROTESTANTS AND NEGROES: LOUISIANA

UNLIKE most of the South, Louisiana* has a great many Roman Catholics of French origin among its citizens. In the areas they inhabit—25 parishes (i.e., counties) in the southern part of the state—the political status of Negroes differs markedly from that in Louisiana's Protestant areas. By 1956 about 51 per cent of potential Negro voters in the Catholic parishes were actually registered; in the white Protestant ones only 23 per cent were.[1] So large a divergence can hardly be due to the rather slight difference in the proportionate size of the Negro population (32 per cent in the French parishes, 38 in the Anglo-American). More plausibly it might be viewed as an instance of the "spiritually equal" status accorded to Negroes in communities with a Catholic tradition.[2] Unfortunately, the topic cannot be explored in the compass of the present inquiry. A large-scale study of Louisiana politics, taking account of the state's ethnic diversity, would likely prove informative.

In the South as a whole Nixon fared much better than Eisenhower had done four years earlier; in Louisiana, on the other hand, Kennedy's vote was almost 25 per cent greater than Eisenhower's had been. Parishes where about 35 per cent of the voters were Catholics went to Kennedy with approximately 65 per cent of their vote. Where Catholics were more numerous, his percentage was correspondingly larger.[3] Catholic parishes with large Negro

---

*Professor James P. Shenton of Columbia University very kindly shared his information and sources with us.

[1]John H. Fenton and Kenneth N. Vines, "Negro Registration in Louisiana," *American Political Science Review*, LI (1957), 706.

[2]This explanation is suggested in *ibid.*, p. 713; cf. Stanley M. Elkins, *Slavery, A Problem in American Institutional and Intellectual Life* (Chicago: University of Chicago Press, 1959), pp. 52-80.

[3]These and the following data were reported by James P. Shenton of Columbia University, in his 1960 Dean's Day lecture at Columbia College (subsequently broadcast over Station WKCR). Professor Shenton informed us that his data were from the research unit of the Republican National Committee, which, in turn, referred us to *Churches and Church Membership in the United States* (New York: National Council of the Churches of Christ in the U.S.A., 1956) for data on the distribution of religious groups in the state, and to population figures released in 1958 by the Louisiana Department of Health for information on Negro and white population and voter registration.

populations voted heavily for Kennedy, sometimes in excess of 80 per cent. In contrast, the strongly Fundamentalist city of Shreveport (located in Caddo, the state's northwesternmost parish) gave Nixon as much as 60 to 65 per cent of the vote in middle-class districts, though less in working-class neighborhoods. All over the state, lower-class Protestant areas having only small numbers of Negroes leaned toward Kennedy; where Negroes were more numerous, most of the white voters supported Nixon, while Kennedy was favored among the Negroes.

The so-called States' Rights vote was more significant in Louisiana than in most other parts of the South. Before the election the States' Rights party was not pledged to any candidate; it sought to attract voters who were rightist in their social and economic views and strongly opposed to the civil-rights planks in the platforms of both major parties. Of just over 800,000 votes in Louisiana, approximately 170,000, more than 20 per cent of the total, were cast for electors of the States' Rights party. The concentration was somewhat higher in the Anglo-American parishes than in the French. The latter, with one-third of the state's population, furnished less than 29 per cent of the party's support. But whether the States' Rights ballots are included or excluded, Kennedy emerges as a favorite in the French regions and a relatively unpopular figure elsewhere. Of the total vote, more than two-thirds went to him in the French parishes and only 40 per cent in the Anglo-American; of the major-party vote, 80 per cent in the former and 52 in the latter.

8. LUTHERAN AND CATHOLIC COUNTIES: MINNESOTA

How Lutherans of German and Scandinavian extraction responded to the religious issue in the 1960 election may be seen in several Minnesota* counties, where voters of this background are heavily concentrated. The state also has overwhelmingly Catholic rural counties, whose response to the religious issue is worth noting. The subject is particularly interesting in view of the historic conflict between Lutheranism and Catholicism.

Lutheran Counties

In fifteen of Minnesota's counties at least 64 per cent of church members are Lutherans. In each, total Protestant church membership is 81.5 per cent or higher.[1] The counties are mostly agricultural and not very populous. Some have small cities with modest industry and commerce, but the commercial firms for the most part serve only the surrounding farm communities. These characteristics are important for the present study because, as we shall see, discontent in farming regions has greatly affected Minnesota politics during the postwar years.

Since the fifteen counties are similar in general character and political behavior, they need not all be examined in complete detail. What follows is a simplified account in which full data are tabulated for only ten—all located in the 7th and 9th Congressional districts, and extending almost the full length of the western side of the state. Those omitted (Chisago, Fillmore, Goodhue, Sibley and Watonwan counties) are in the south and southeast.

Table 15 reports the Democratic vote in selected elections since 1928. As the figures show, most of the ten counties appear to

*We are grateful to Sidney S. Goldish, director of research for the Minneapolis *Star* and *Tribune,* for data and information.

[1]Data from the National Council of the Churches of Christ in the U.S.A., *op. cit.* These statistics may actually understate the Protestant share of the population, because the criteria used by Protestant denominations to determine membership apparently are more rigorous and restrictive than those of the Catholic church. Quite possibly, many persons who are not members of a Lutheran congregation ought yet to be counted as Lutherans for the purpose of this study; unfortunately, there are no data on which such a count might be based.

be normally Democratic. Only Otter Tail is clearly Republican, though some others occasionally cross over. In 1928, however, not one went to Smith—surely an indication how strong religious considerations then were in these counties. This indication is confirmed by the region's massive vote for Roosevelt four years later. The local returns in 1932 amounted to an upheaval of staggering proportions, even larger than might be expected in a time of economic depression and chaos, when the nation was anxious for a change in Washington. While in the state as a whole the shift to the Democrats was just under 21 per cent (from 41.4 per cent for Smith to 62.3 per cent for Roosevelt), here the Democratic gains ranged from 24.3 per cent in Otter Tail County to 43.5 in Norman.

Even a cursory comparison of the 1928 and 1932 figures with those of 1960 shows that the religious factor was much less important here in the latter year. In fact, Kennedy carried six of the ten counties. He fared badly only in heavily Republican Otter Tail, and even there less poorly than Smith. In the five counties not included in Table 15, all traditionally Republican, Kennedy did not do well; but here, too, except in one county, his percentages were above Smith's.[2] Thus, religious prejudice or tension in the area seems to have lessened remarkably in the generation between the two presidential elections with Catholic candidates.

At first sight the figures might nevertheless seem to indicate at least a vestige of the religious factor, in that Kennedy won only about the same proportion of the vote as Stevenson in 1956, except in Kittson and Lac qui Parle counties. Since Stevenson had been running against an unusually popular opponent, Kennedy's failure to improve on his performance might suggest a certain coolness among the voters—a coolness which might conceivably derive from religious considerations. But this first impression does

---

[2]The exception is Sibley County. Comparative Democratic percentages follow:

County	1928 (Smith)	1932 (Roosevelt)	1960 (Kennedy)
Chisago	23.5	54.7	43.2
Fillmore	21.7	50.9	34.3
Goodhue	26.5	57.6	34.9
Sibley	43.6	77.3	33.8
Watonwan	29.9	59.3	36.6

TABLE 15

DEMOCRATIC VOTE IN TEN PREDOMINANTLY LUTHERAN COUNTIES IN MINNESOTA, 1928, 1932, 1948-1960

(Per cent)

County	President 1928 (Smith)	President 1932 (Roosevelt)	President 1948 (Truman)	President 1952 (Stevenson)	Governor 1954 (Freeman)	Senator 1954 (Humphrey)	President 1956 (Stevenson)	Governor 1956 (Freeman)	Governor 1958 (Freeman)	Senator 1958 (McCarthy)	President 1960 (Kennedy)	Governor 1960 (Freeman)	Senator 1960 (Humphrey)
Chippewa	36.4	66.7	60.2	41.8	51.5	57.0	48.7	53.3	57.0	50.1	48.2	49.7	55.9
Clearwater	38.5	76.1	70.5	51.5	64.6	70.5	59.7	65.0	70.2	62.7	59.9	61.8	68.5
Grant	45.1	70.2	57.1	40.2	53.3	60.6	50.5	54.7	56.7	52.0	51.0	51.7	58.7
Kittson	41.4	71.1	74.2	56.5	66.9	73.4	58.6	67.9	71.3	57.8	53.4	61.7	63.7
Lac qui Parle	39.7	67.6	61.3	41.2	50.1	57.3	46.3	52.0	56.7	49.8	50.5	48.5	56.5
Norman	29.8	73.3	65.7	44.5	56.5	64.8	54.0	62.1	67.1	59.3	52.6	57.9	63.9
Otter Tail	30.0	54.3	37.0	24.7	38.1	42.6	34.0	37.9	40.4	36.3	36.9	36.5	42.2
Pennington	32.3	69.4	65.9	50.7	60.9	69.6	55.0	62.8	69.3	61.9	55.6	60.8	65.9
Pope	33.0	67.9	60.6	39.9	53.8	58.8	48.6	52.3	56.8	49.4	48.5	50.6	57.0
Yellow Medicine	46.4	72.5	60.7	42.1	53.3	58.4	48.7	52.4	57.9	50.8	48.9	49.2	55.9
Total State	41.4	62.3	58.9	44.4	53.0	57.2	46.2	51.6	57.3	53.2	50.9	49.1	57.5

Source: Computed from Governmental Affairs Institute, *op. cit.*; the *World Almanac*; Minneapolis *Morning Tribune*, November 9, 1960.

not stand up under closer inspection. In 1956, contrary to the national trend, Eisenhower had lost some of his Minnesota support; his vote fell off by 1.8 per cent in the state as a whole, and by more than that in each of the ten Lutheran counties. Stevenson's gains ranged from 2.1 per cent in Kittson County to more than 10 per cent in Grant, with most of the rest on the high side of this range. Thus the effect of Eisenhower's special popularity had already been eliminated in these counties by 1960.[3]

As has been noted, the counties under study are a farm and dairy region, and the past few years have been very difficult for them. Farm conditions are a major factor in Minnesota voting.[4] Thus in 1956, under a Republican administration, discontent in Minnesota farming regions redounded to the advantage of the Democrats. Eight years earlier the farm vote had been an important component of Harry S. Truman's unexpected victory. Truman carried Minnesota by the largest plurality in a generation except those for Roosevelt in 1932 and 1936, and in the Lutheran counties, except Otter Tail, he did very well indeed. We may therefore conclude that in 1960, as before, voters in these counties were prompted more by what they considered to be their economic needs than by whatever religious prejudice may have survived among them.

Statewide voting returns over the years show that the margins of the Democrats' frequent victories vary conspicuously. Under the most favorable circumstances, a Democratic candidate for state office may hope to poll somewhat over 57 per cent of the vote (though Truman did even better in 1948). Presumably this is the approximate limit of reasonable Democratic aspiration, reached only under unusual circumstances or by an exceptionally attractive candidate. Senator Hubert H. Humphrey, a highly popular leader in the state, won both of his campaigns for reelection to the Senate with about 57 per cent. Former Governor Orville L. Free-

---

[3]Sidney S. Goldish notes in a letter dated June 30, 1961, that Kennedy was about 4.5 per cent ahead of Stevenson in the state at large, and that none of the fifteen Lutheran counties came up to that figure. But this argument fails to take account of the fact that these counties had already made a larger shift toward the Democrats in 1956 than the state as a whole.
[4]This point was also emphasized in Goldish's letter.

man attained the maximum only once—in 1958, a year when he is believed to have benefited from farm discontent.[5] Previously he had not been sufficiently well known to achieve so large a plurality; and by 1960, according to press interpretations of Minnesota politics, his six years in office had given him opportunities to step on so many toes that he was narrowly defeated.

In most of the Lutheran counties the Democrats' peak years, as well as their less dramatic ones, have coincided with those in the state at large (Table 15). Thus Kennedy, who barely managed to squeeze through in the state, also did only moderately well in the ten counties taken together, staying far below the maximum reasonable expectation. Freeman, though the loser in the state, ran ahead of Kennedy in eight of the ten counties; and Humphrey, who achieved the maximum in the state, outran both in all ten. It may be that Kennedy was somewhat handicapped by his religion, but on the other hand there seems to be no reason why he should have been as popular in Minnesota as the state's senior Senator.

In short, whether a candidate achieves the maximum reasonable expectation for Minnesota depends so much on personal popularity and economic conditions that Kennedy's falling short of the mark cannot definitely be put down to anti-Catholic prejudice. His and Senator McCarthy's future performance in the Lutheran counties should be instructive, particularly if economic conditions are good and the nation is not confronted by war.

Catholic Counties

Catholics constitute 63.0 to 79.6 per cent of church members in six Minnesota counties: Benton, Mahnoman, Morrison, Red Lake, Scott and Stearns.[6] These counties, like those just discussed, are agricultural and sparsely populated areas. Their voting data are summarized in Table 16; the same elections are included as above.

---

[5]The farm problem also seems to have contributed to Senator Eugene McCarthy's comfortable though not overwhelming victory that year. McCarthy, like Kennedy, is a Catholic, and was then running against a Lutheran incumbent, but this fact does not seem to have hurt him in the Lutheran counties. If he trailed Freeman, the probable reason is simply that it was his first statewide candidacy, while Freeman was widely known across the state.

[6]National Council of the Churches of Christ in the U.S.A., *op. cit.*

TABLE 16

DEMOCRATIC VOTE IN SIX PREDOMINANTLY CATHOLIC COUNTIES IN MINNESOTA, 1928, 1932, 1948-1960

(Per cent)

County	1928 President (Smith)	1932 President (Roosevelt)	1948 President (Truman)	1952 President (Stevenson)	1954 Governor (Freeman)	1954 Senator (Humphrey)	1956 President (Stevenson)	1956 Governor (Freeman)	1958 Governor (Freeman)	1958 Senator (McCarthy)	1960 President (Kennedy)	1960 Governor (Freeman)	1960 Senator (Humphrey)
Mahnoman	69.5	86.8	78.6	54.1	67.4	73.6	63.4	69.3	71.3	68.6	67.9	53.8	70.5
Red Lake	67.9	84.4	74.9	58.1	71.9	77.8	66.5	71.1	74.7	70.7	73.3	70.6	78.2
Benton	53.5	74.6	63.1	40.2	50.4	56.8	42.1	45.7	55.3	55.8	55.8	46.0	57.9
Morrison	57.6	75.3	60.6	42.9	57.1	60.8	48.0	52.3	57.3	58.7	62.4	55.1	62.4
Scott	71.8	81.1	62.4	43.7	58.4	61.6	45.3	52.3	60.6	57.7	62.3	54.0	62.3
Stearns	71.4	80.3	60.0	35.2	49.8	55.0	36.1	42.7	51.3	55.3	58.3	45.0	55.7

Source: Computed from Governmental Affairs Institute, *op. cit.*; the *World Almanac*; Minneapolis *Morning Tribune*, November 9, 1960.

As the table shows, the counties fall into two distinct groups. Mahnoman and Red Lake are traditionally Democratic. The remaining four incline the other way: they went Republican in both of the Eisenhower-Stevenson elections, as well as in Roosevelt's last two (not included in the table), though on many other occasions they have given majorities—even heavy majorities—to Democratic candidates. We may reasonably think of them as more or less Republican, though far from hidebound in their party adherence.

In 1928 all six of the Catholic counties supported Al Smith, and four years later all six supported Roosevelt even more strongly.[7] It would seem, then, that the voters a generation ago were responsive both to the religious issue and to the critically important economic questions of the time—sufficiently so in both instances to overcome their ordinary political preference.

In 1948, presumably because of the farm problem, all six voted overwhelmingly for Truman, with the two Democratic counties far ahead of the rest. Subsequently, as noted above, the four Republican counties returned to their normal political loyalty and supported Eisenhower both times; but, again contrary to the nation at large, Stevenson gained throughout the six in 1956. Though Stevenson is widely thought to have aroused antipathy among Catholics, he did reasonably well in the two normally Democratic counties in 1952, and very well in 1956, with 63.4 in one and 66.5 per cent in the other. Still, remarkable as his success may seem, the two counties have voted even more heavily for other Democratic candidates.

All six counties—again especially the Democratic ones—favored Senator Eugene McCaɪʎhy in 1958. This outcome might seem to be due to the religious issue, except that Freeman, running for re-election as Governor, polled about the same number of votes. Indeed, Freeman ran a few points ahead not only in the two Democratic counties but also in one of the others. His strength in normally Republican counties again suggests that the plight of

---

[7]They also supported Roosevelt in 1936 but, contrary to the national trend, in decreased numbers. In Scott and Stearns counties, the Roosevelt vote fell off by almost 10 per cent and in Benton County by 11 per cent.

Minnesota agriculture was a factor in the 1958 election. There is thus little ground for claiming that in backing McCarthy Catholic voters simply voted for one of their own.

Any interpretation of the Kennedy vote in these counties as merely a reaction to the religious issue leads to similar difficulties, even though religion does seem to have exerted some influence. Kennedy did very well here; his percentage was consistently greater than Stevenson's had been in 1952, and in the Republican counties it was very much greater. Indeed, he was about as successful as the most popular Democratic candidates for state office. Thus, he ran slightly behind Humphrey in three counties (including the two Democratic ones), about even with him in two, and slightly ahead in one. (Similar results emerge when his showing is compared with Humphrey's in 1954 or Freeman's in 1958.) In other words, the Catholic counties, unlike the Lutheran, gave Kennedy enough support to attain what was described above as the maximum reasonable expectation for a Democratic candidate. His Catholicism may fairly be viewed as a factor in this achievement. But it would be a mistake to see it as the sole factor, or to lay a great deal of stress on it, since non-Catholic Democrats have also achieved the maximum in these counties.

Thus, in neither the Catholic nor the Protestant counties studied in rural Minnesota does the religious issue seem to have been of pressing importance. It did not seriously affect the voters, who continued to act on the assumption that economic interests are paramount in politics.

Jewish Voting Behavior

9. SUBURBS AND NEAR-SUBURBS

CONSIDERABLE information about the way Jews in the large cities have voted has already been accumulated. But with the breakup of the old urban neighborhoods and the continuous outward movement of Jews to the city's outer rings and the suburbs, we were interested to learn to what extent Jews in these newer areas retained their party loyalties and old voting habits. We selected three such areas: in the metropolitan Chicago, New York, and Detroit.

Chicago: Ward 50 and Suburbs*

Located on the North Side just within the city limits, Chicago's Ward 50 is roughly coextensive with the West Ridge district, popularly known as West Rogers Park. For the last decade the area has been in transition, with Jews moving in and Christians moving out. In 1951 about 11,200 Jews lived there; six years later, 17,800.[1] The Jewish concentration has become so high that it appeared to an analyst of neighborhood change as the outcome of a desire to create a Jewish community, maintain its special institutions and halt assimilation.[2]

Ward 50 traditionally has been middle class, populated mostly by Irish Catholics and Scandinavian and German Protestants. In 1960 voter-registration lists showed that Jews had settled chiefly in formerly Irish precincts, while some of the Scandinavian and Scandinavian-German precincts still had few Jewish newcomers. But both the Scandinavians and the Irish have been departing fairly rapidly from Ward 50. The extent of the Christian exodus and the Jewish influx is illustrated by the sale, in 1959, of a Lutheran church building to the Workmen's Circle.[3] This Yiddishist, secular,

---

*Dr. Walter P. Zand, director of the American Jewish Committee's Chicago office, was most helpful in providing us with a variety of useful materials.
[1] Esther Beckenstein, *Report on the Jewish Population of Metropolitan Chicago* (Chicago: Jewish Federation of Metropolitan Chicago, May 1959), p. 10.
[2] Erich Rosenthal, "Acculturation without Assimilation: The Jewish Community of Chicago, Illinois," *American Journal of Sociology*, LXVI (1960), 275-288.
[3] *Idem*, "This Was North Lawndale: The Transplantation of a Jewish Community," *Jewish Social Studies*, XXII (1960), 77.

labor-oriented fraternal society requires a highly dense Jewish neighborhood from which to draw its membership.

TABLE 17

REPUBLICAN VOTE IN WARD 50 AND CHICAGO, 1950-1956

(Per cent)

Election	Ward 50	Total city
Senator, 1950	63.1	45.7
Governor, 1952	52.6	43.6
President, 1952	56.4	45.6
Senator, 1954	43.0	35.8
Senator, 1956	43.1	45.5
Governor, 1956	61.1	41.9
President, 1956	52.1	51.3

Source: Governmental Affairs Institute, *op. cit.*

In the past, Ward 50 voted Republican more frequently than the city at large, as shown in Table 17, which gives the Republican vote from 1950 to 1956. But the pattern has been somewhat erratic, either as a result of local and regional factors or because of the opposing tendencies of Irish Catholic Democrats and Scandinavian or German Protestant Republicans. In 1960 the ward went strongly for the Kennedy ticket, its Democratic percentage rising higher than its Republican percentages for the corresponding offices in the past, and about as high as the Democratic vote in the city as a whole (Table 18).

How are we to account for this Democratic sweep? The presidential vote might be explained by Nixon's lack of appeal for independent voters or by the attraction of Kennedy's religion for the Catholics, but this would not account for the other contests. Were ethnic influences at work? Table 19 isolates some group factors in the ward, by comparing presidential votes (1956 and 1960) in two sets of predominantly Jewish precincts with those in a group of Scandinavian and German ones. The figures demonstrate a consistent Democratic preference among Jews, confirming a survey made early in 1956, which found 84 per cent of the Jews interviewed in Ward 50 strongly or moderately Democratic, as against 36 per cent of the Catholics and 21 per cent of the Protestants.[4] The increased Democratic percentage in 1960, in the Jewish

TABLE 18

DEMOCRATIC VOTE IN WARD 50 AND CHICAGO, 1960

(Per cent)

Office	Ward 50	Total city
President	62.3	61.7
Senator	66.0	66.3
Governor	69.0	66.0
State's Attorney	56.1	57.0
Coroner	61.6	62.6

Source: Computed from election returns in the Chicago *Tribune*, November 10, 1960.

TABLE 19

DEMOCRATIC VOTE FOR PRESIDENT IN SELECTED JEWISH AND SCANDINAVIAN PRECINCTS IN WARD 50, CHICAGO 1956 AND 1960

(Per cent)

Area	Presidential 1956	Presidential 1960
Total ward	47.9	62.3
6 Scandinavian and Scandinavian-German precincts	30.1	38.3
6 precincts, 80-90 per cent Jewish	75.9	82.4
15 precincts, 65-75 per cent Jewish	74.7	77.8

Source: Computed from official returns obtained from the Board of Elections of Cook County, Ill. Ethnic densities estimated on the basis of voter-registration lists.

[4]Maurice G. Guysenir, "Jewish Vote in Chicago," *Jewish Social Studies,* XX (1958), 208.

precincts and consequently in the ward as a whole, would thus seem to be due to the increased number of Jewish voters, rather than to Nixon's being less popular then Eisenhower.

Table 19 further suggests that the religious issue was not significant among the ward's Scandinavians and Germans, most of whom are Lutherans.[5] They gave Kennedy more votes than they had given Stevenson—or Nixon fewer than they had given Eisenhower.

City and suburban returns in the Chicago area indicate that a rise in socio-economic status tends to reduce the Democratic vote among Jews. Ward 50 showed this trend in 1952, when 38 per cent

TABLE 20

DEMOCRATIC VOTE IN JEWISH AND OTHER PRECINCTS
OF CHICAGO SUBURBS, 1960

(Per cent)

Middle-class (Skokie)

1 precinct, 80 per cent Jewish (Mostly tenants in apartments)	72.6
1 precinct, nearly half Jewish (Average value of home $25,000)	49.2
2 precincts, 15 per cent Jewish (Average value of home $25,000)	27.4

Middle-class (Wilmette and Glenview)
(Average value of home $30,000)

1 precinct, 75 per cent Jewish	63.8
1 precinct, 25 per cent Jewish	30.1
1 precinct, not Jewish	19.7

Upper-middle-class (Highland Park)
(Average value of home $35,000)

1 precinct, 70 per cent Jewish	51.8
2 precincts, 75 per cent Protestant	38.0

Source: Computed from official returns obtained from the Board of Elections of Cook and Lake Counties, Ill.

---

[5] *Ibid.*, p. 209.

of Jews in the high socio-economic bracket voted for Eisenhower, as against 27 per cent in the middle and 5 per cent in the low bracket.[6] Tables 20 and 21 illustrate the same phenomenon in greater detail, on the basis of returns from both city and suburban areas. The Democratic percentage in Jewish neighborhoods consistently decreases as we move from lower to higher socio-economic levels. But, as Table 20 indicates, the Democratic vote among middle-class and upper-middle-class Jews still is much higher than among others of equal status.

TABLE 21

DEMOCRATIC VOTE IN PRECINCTS 70 TO 80 PER CENT JEWISH, BY ECONOMIC RANK, IN AND NEAR CHICAGO, 1960

(Per cent)

1. *Lower-middle* (city) 4 precincts in Ward 40	85.8
2. *Middle* (city limits) 15 precincts in Ward 50	77.8
3. *Middle* (suburban; tenants) 1 precinct in Skokie	72.6
4. *Middle* (suburban; $30,000 homes) 1 precinct in Wilmette	63.8
5. *Upper* (suburban; $35,000 homes) 1 precinct in Highland Park	51.8

Source: Computed from official returns obtained from the Board of Elections of Cook County, Ill.; Nisson Gross, Anti-Defamation League, Chicago office; Highland Park *News*, November 24, 1960.

Near New York: Great Neck

Great Neck, a community on Long Island just outside New York City, is part of the 3rd Assembly District of Republican Nassau County. Its population, containing one of the highest concentrations of Jews in the county, is for the most part prosperous. Yet, despite its affluence and its Republican environment, Great Neck did not go to Nixon.

In the community as a whole, Kennedy received 10,900 votes

[6]*Ibid.*, pp. 200f.

(54.8 per cent) on the Democratic and Liberal lines,[7] as against 8,988 for Nixon. In ten election districts shown by their registration lists to be heavily Jewish, Kennedy received 4,514 votes (61.1 per cent) out of 7,384. Outside these ten districts, he won 6,386 votes (51.1 per cent) to Nixon's 6,118. It must be remembered that the latter districts, though not overwhelmingly Jewish like the former, yet have many Jewish residents; none is without Jews.

Findings for Great Neck, then, would seem to be similar to those for the Chicago suburb of Highland Park. In Great Neck well-to-do, very heavily Jewish areas gave Kennedy about 60 per cent of their vote; in Highland Park, similar areas, but with a less solidly Jewish population (about 70 per cent), gave him somewhat more than 50 per cent.

Near Detroit: Oak Park and Harper Woods

A Michigan poll sponsored by the Detroit *News* the week before the 1960 election predicted that Kennedy would receive 52.9 per cent of the vote, and that John B. Swainson, the Democratic candidate for Governor, would win with 51.5 per cent.[8] The *News* poll found support for Kennedy strongest among Jewish respondents—89.7 per cent. No other group, whether classified by religion or by race, age, occupation, residence or birth, was so solidly Democratic.[9] Negroes were next, with 82.9 per cent, and Catholics third, with 77.9 per cent. Groups 60 to 70 per cent for Kennedy were unskilled labor, craftsmen and foremen, foreign-born persons, and renters. Nixon's supporters were primarily rural; they

---

[7]Computations for Great Neck are based on the vote of the Democratic, Liberal and Republican parties; splinter parties are not included. The returns for Kennedy are totals of Democratic and Liberal votes.

[8]Published in the *News* on November 6, 1960. The poll was the last in a series of four conducted for the *News* by Richard W. Oudersluy's Market Opinion Research Company. Its reliability is attested by the accuracy with which it forecast the outcome. The actual statewide vote for Kennedy was 50.9 per cent, that for Swainson 51.3 per cent.

[9]This finding is confirmed in an analysis by the Jewish Community Council of Detroit, based on estimates of Jewish population made for the Jewish Welfare Federation by Professor Albert J. Mayer of Wayne State University, director of the Detroit Area Traffic Study. Six precincts in Detroit's Ward 16, about 80 per cent Jewish, were found to have voted 81.9 per cent for Kennedy. Eighteen precincts in the same ward, about 60 per cent Jewish, gave Kennedy 73.3 per cent of their vote.

included more than 70 per cent of farm owners, managers, laborers and hired hands. Nearly 65 per cent of respondents more than sixty years old were for Nixon, as were 59 per cent of Protestants.

The Detroit *News* poll showed the familiar ingredients of the Democratic coalition: urban industrial workers (mostly Catholic and, in Detroit, of East or South European birth or extraction), Negroes, Jews, tenants and the poor. This was particularly evident in Wayne County, i.e., the Detroit metropolitan area. The county's Democratic plurality of nearly 400,000 votes—about 200,000 more than Stevenson's in 1956—was just large enough to overcome Nixon's lead in the rest of the state, and for the first time since 1944 Michigan went to a Democratic presidential candidate. But the poll results would scarcely justify the conclusion that Kennedy's religion was a major factor in this outcome. The Detroit area, where workers and trade unionists predominate, has been Democratic territory for decades; and here, as in Buffalo, the categories of union membership, Catholicism and adherence to the Democratic party overlap, so that economic and religious factors cannot be readily separated. For the most part the increased Democratic plurality probably should be attributed to rising unemployment in the area's major industry.

The religious factor does seem to have played a role in some of Detroit's middle-class suburbs. This conclusion is suggested by an analysis of data from two communities, Oak Park and Harper Woods, where shortly before the elections Wayne State University social scientists interviewed more than 500 voters in the course of a survey of local political issues.[10]

Oak Park adjoins the Northwest section of Detroit proper, a district where the Jewish population has been concentrating in the last decade. Many of the city's younger Jewish families have been moving into both areas from earlier Jewish neighborhoods, where Negroes are now settling. As Jews have moved into Oak Park, many Christians have moved away. At the time of the Wayne State University sampling, nearly 60 per cent of the population was Jewish, about 25 per cent Protestant and about 12 per cent

---

[10]Professor Mayer most generously made available to us the IBM cards for this study, as well as his time and his perceptive understanding.

Catholic. Well over 80 per cent of the Jews in Oak Park are immigrants or children of immigrants from Eastern Europe, particularly Poland and Russia; only 4 per cent are of German background. Among the Christians national ancestry is more varied. Of the Protestants, about 57 per cent are British or Scandinavian, and about 22 per cent are German; of the Catholics, Poles account for 21 per cent, Germans for 16, and Irish and Italians each for 14 per cent.

Harper Woods, a northeastern suburb, has practically no Jews. Catholics are a bare majority of 52 per cent. The largest Protestant denomination is the Lutheran, with nearly 20 per cent of the population. Income and education levels are higher in Oak Park than in Harper Woods, the Jews standing highest in each category. In both suburbs, Catholics were found to have higher incomes than Protestants—the reverse of what has been found in Detroit itself.[11]

In the Wayne State University survey, 78 per cent of the Oak Park respondents said they would vote for Kennedy; the area's actual vote for him was 76 per cent. In Harper Woods 58 per cent said they would vote for him; 63 per cent did. The difference may be due to shifts in attitude between the time of the survey and Election Day. As was to be expected, the survey found Catholics and Jews predominantly for Kennedy and Protestants mostly for Nixon. But, surprisingly, marked differences were revealed between the Catholics in Oak Park and those in Harper Woods, as well as between the Protestants in the two suburbs. As Table 22 shows, respondents in Harper Woods were sharply divided along religious lines, with 88 per cent of Catholics for Kennedy and 80 per cent of Protestants for Nixon. No such marked cleavage was found in Oak Park. In 1956 Catholics in both suburbs had split nearly evenly between both parties, while more Protestants in Harper Woods voted Democratic in 1956 than in 1960.

Are the differences between the 1960 voting patterns in the two communities linked in any way to the large number of Jews in Oak Park and their virtual absence in Harper Woods? Possibly the Protestants and Catholics who chose to remain in Oak Park

---

[11]Cf. Lenski, *op. cit.,* pp. 79-81.

TABLE 22

1960 PRESIDENTIAL CHOICE AND 1956 PRESIDENTIAL VOTE,
BY RELIGION, IN TWO DETROIT SUBURBS

(Per cent)

Religious group	Suburb	1960 choice		1956 vote	
		Nixon	Kennedy	Eisenhower	Stevenson
Catholics	Oak Park	29	71	51	49
	Harper Woods	12	88	48	52
Protestants	Oak Park	53	47	63	37
	Harper Woods	80	20	74	26
Jews	Oak Park	7	93	14	86

Source: Computed from data on IBM cards.

after the heavy Jewish influx are particularly free from ethnic and religious prejudice. Can this attitude be translated into political terms and support for a particular party? The Republicans have often been viewed as spokesmen of that once dominant rural and small-town native Protestant American culture which sees virtue only on the farm and nothing but vice and corruption in the cities. In those cities live the foreigners, the immigrants, the Negroes. The Democrats, for their part, have always particularly appealed to those minority groups and enjoyed their support. Conceivably, then, voters who are open-minded about minorities might be more responsive to the Democratic party.

Thus a strong, consistent Democratic preference in a given community might serve as a rough indicator of a relatively un-prejudiced or open-minded climate. But the data do not support this hypothesis: while the Protestants in Oak Park were more Democratic than their counterparts in Harper Woods, the Catholics were less so. Perhaps the open-mindedness of Christians in Oak Park expressed itself in freedom from the rigid Catholic-Demo-cratic and Protestant-Republican alignments typical of Harper Woods (Table 22), rather than in consistent preference for one party.

Alternately, the presence of Jews in Oak Park may have had

a more direct effect on the voting of Christians. At the outset, Jews in the community strongly favored Stevenson; 76 per cent of Jewish respondents to the Wayne State University survey named him as their choice in the Democratic presidential primary (Table 23). Kennedy at first was supported mainly by Catholics. At the

TABLE 23

PRESIDENTIAL CHOICES IN 1960 DEMOCRATIC PRIMARY, BY RELIGION, IN OAK PARK

(Per cent)

Religious group	Stevenson	Kennedy	Other
Catholics	27	64	9
Protestants	55	29	16
Jews	76	17	7

Source: Computed from data on IBM cards.

time of the primary, only 29 per cent of the Protestants and 17 per cent of the Jews favored his candidacy. But after overcoming their disappointment over Stevenson's primary defeat, Jewish voters in Oak Park began to support Kennedy intensely and often vociferously. Their new position probably helped local Protestants realize that Kennedy was, as he expressed it, "not the Catholic candidate" but the Democratic candidate, and thus minimized anti-Catholicism as a factor in the election. This in turn may have made it possible for Oak Park's Catholics to feel less embattled, less driven to vote Democratic merely as a rebuke to bigotry, and freer to make their choice on other grounds. But in Harper Woods, with no Jews to influence them, Catholics and Protestants expressed their mutual apprehensions in a highly rigid political fashion, with nearly all Catholics voting Democratic and nearly all Protestants Republican.

10. SPECIAL APPEALS TO JEWISH VOTERS

ATTEMPTS to influence the vote of minority groups by appealing to their interests and fears are a well-known feature of American political life. In the preceding chapters we have sought to explore how members of such groups vote; we will now concern ourselves with the appeals made to some of them.

On the seamy side of the 1960 campaign, religion was often an issue. Specifically, a good deal of propaganda was addressed to Protestants' fears and prejudices concerning the Catholic Church and its communicants.[1] In addition, voters of Irish, Italian, Polish and other extraction were told that this or that candidate was especially attuned to their interests or the needs of "the old country."[2]

Both parties customarily establish so-called nationality committees to deal with the special problems presented by the voters of the ethnic and religious minorities,[3] and recruit workers who supposedly know just how to appeal to each of these groups. It is assumed that different minorities require different procedures or styles of operation, depending in some measure, one may suspect, on their success in America to date.

At one extreme one finds completely unsophisticated exhortations urging voters of nationality X to vote for a given candidate because he, too, is of X ancestry. At the other, the candidate need not be of the same extraction as the group to which the appeal is directed. It is enough to publish an advertisement of a general nature, containing only passing references to the group's special interests, and signed mostly, though not exclusively, by members of the group.

Attempts to influence Jewish voters are more likely to be of the subtle than the obvious kind, though examples run the entire

---

[1] For a survey of this material, see Fair Campaign Practices Committee, *The State-by-State Study of Smear: 1960; Report* (New York, February 1962), 16 pp., processed.

[2] Moses Rischin, *"Our Own Kind": Voting by Race, Creed or National Origin* (Santa Barbara, Calif.: Center for the Study of Democratic Institutions, 1960), pp. 15-23, discusses this aspect of the 1956 campaign.

[3] For a survey of how this is done, see "Parties Vie for Vote of Ethnic American," *Congressional Quarterly,* week ending November 4, 1960, pp. 1839-1846.

gamut. In 1960, it has been said, the Democratic plan of action was to appeal to the Jews by indirection, through emphasis on liberal causes they were known to favor; the Republican strategy was more direct.[4]

The specific subjects of political appeals to the Jewish group usually are anti-Semitism and Israel. Invariably a candidate's stand on both issues is proclaimed to be "good for the Jews," whereas his opponent's is said to be at best doubtful. There may be other issues as well, but on closer inspection they often turn out to be variations on the main themes. For example, in addressing a Jewish audience, party spokesmen may emphasize their candidate's opposition to the McCarran-Walter Act and his support of liberalized immigration laws. The candidate is thereby accredited as a man of liberal principles before an audience known to favor liberal candidates; but, more important, the attack on a discriminatory law, with its implications of group inferiority, serves as a token of his personal good will toward minority groups in general and as an indirect disavowal of anti-Semitism.

In 1960 the theme of anti-Semitism was repeatedly sounded. Nixon was often charged with being an anti-Semite, even though he had never betrayed animosity toward Jews in any way. Because of the total lack of evidence, no responsible person in the opposite camp could permit himself or his party to be named as an official source for this allegation; yet the charge was permitted to circulate. For example, the fact that Nixon had signed a restrictive covenant when he bought his Washington home was widely publicized. The intent obviously was to discredit him, not to denounce housing discrimination; for in retailing the story no one discussed the circumstances of house buying in Washington, no one asked whether Nixon had been aware of the restrictive clause, and no one pointed out that such covenants have no standing in court and are unenforceable.

To answer inquiries occasioned by rumors like these, Jewish organizations, having investigated the matter, dismissed charges of anti-Semitism against Nixon as unfounded. At the same time,

[4]Roma Lipsky, "Electioneering Among the Minorities," *Commentary*, May 1961, pp. 428-432.

partisan efforts were made to turn the smear into a plea for sympathy and for votes—for example, in an advertisement signed "Friends of Nixon-Lodge" in the Detroit *Jewish News* (October 28). The layout featured a picture of an old man with a skullcap, long gray hair and beard, and a large, presumably rabbinical, book open before him. Underneath, a headline asked: "Have we forgotten the Ninth Commandment?" The text opened with the words of the commandment against bearing false witness; further down, the advertisement praised Nixon and called upon Kennedy to repudiate the slander lest he appear willing to profit from it. At the end the sponsors urged voters to support Nixon and Lodge "for their contributions to the cause of humanity."

Kennedy was rarely charged with anti-Semitism in so many words, but there were strong hints that he had been raised in an anti-Semitic environment—specifically that his father, Joseph P. Kennedy, onetime United States Ambassador to Great Britain, had sympathized with Hitler. Presumably the purveyors thought this story would appear plausible in view of well-known tensions between Irish and Jews, and would cost Kennedy Jewish votes which a Democratic candidate for President could normally expect to win. A dispatch by Herbert von Dirksen, Hitler's Ambassador to Great Britain, describing the elder Kennedy as sympathetic to Hitler and the Nazi party's anti-Jewish beliefs, was unearthed, and excerpts were widely circulated under various auspices.

One of the incarnations of the story was an open letter, signed by the Lincoln-Dembitz Republican League and published as an advertisement in the *Sentinel,* a Jewish weekly in Chicago. Another was a crude leaflet, published by a "Committee for Human Dignity," with a New York address, which claimed that John Kennedy was very much under paternal influence, with the usual implications about his father. Republicans were not above distributing propaganda of this kind even from official headquarters; at one point in the campaign, two prominent Jewish Republicans from New York, United States Senator Jacob K. Javits and State Attorney General Louis J. Lefkowitz, called a news conference to deplore this practice.[5]

---

[5]New York *Times,* November 5, 1960.

Since few voters could be expected to believe that either candidate was anti-Semitic, Israel emerged as the main ingredient of appeals to Jewish voters in 1960, though less so than in 1956. American Jews for the most part view the State of Israel affectionately or at least sympathetically; to play up to these feelings is an obvious way to seek Jewish votes. Both major parties took account of this fact at the outset, expressing concern for Israel in their platforms.[6] Indeed, the issue was thought too good to be used only on behalf of presidential candidates. Thus it was the main topic of an advertisement for Republican Congressman Lawrence Curtis of Massachusetts, published in the Boston *Jewish Advocate* (October 20). Israel also figured prominently in "Congressman [Emanuel] Celler's Report to His Voters," a statement inserted by the Democrat from New York in the *Congressional Record* (September 1) and distributed by mail.

Partisans on both sides paraded their respective favorites' records on Israel as eminently favorable and, at the same time, impugned those of the opposing candidates. The latter tactic often caused the other side to cry out in hurt and dismay at the lengths to which campaigners would go just to win votes. As usual, major candidates were constantly being called upon by the opposition to repudiate their supporters' excesses.

Of the Republican candidates, Henry Cabot Lodge seems to have been more vigorously attacked as unfriendly to Israel than Nixon. In pressing their case, the Democrats received major support from a syndicated column by Drew Pearson (August 31). Pearson reported that during the 1956 Suez crisis, Lodge, then the United States Ambassador to the United Nations, had strongly urged sanctions against Israel—while Senator Lyndon B. Johnson, now Lodge's opponent for the vice presidency, had insisted that the United States Senate would "never back up any anti-Israel sanctions you may impose in the United Nations," and had wondered why the American Ambassador sounded "more like an Arab spokesman than a diplomat of the United States." Democrats were understandably pleased to make this information available to all; the Great Neck Democratic Club admitted mailing out liter-

---

[6] See *American Jewish Year Book*, LXII (1961), 197f.

ature which said Lodge had "incurred the displeasure of American Zionists for his treatment of Israel when he was Ambassador to the United Nations." [7]

The attack on Lodge was countered in several ways. One of the replies was a leaflet produced in suburban Westchester County, north of New York City, by a group called "Westchester Division, Friends of Nixon and Lodge." The names on the masthead were almost all Jewish. The text listed and refuted charges made against Nixon as well as Lodge, including some concerning Israel. Less defensive and perhaps more widely noted were several flyers with excerpts from Israeli newspapers praising Nixon as a friend of Israel, and criticizing Kennedy as indifferent, or only interested enough to avoid antagonizing the Jewish voters of Massachusetts. A leaflet of this sort was circulated, for example, by a group calling itself "Committee for Human Rights," with a New York address.

Charges against Kennedy consistently stressed indifference to Israel rather than hostility. Among his many international interests, so the argument ran, there simply was no room for Israel. Kennedy's supporters lost no time in denying the charge. One of the replies was a five-page mimeographed communication, signed "New York State Democratic Committee, Committee on Nationalities and Intergroup Relations," yet containing the words "We Jews" on the front page. Almost two pages were devoted to statements by Kennedy illustrating why Jews ought to vote for him; many of the quotations had to do with Israel and the Near East. In Boston a prominent Jew, Fred Monosson, published a full-page advertisement in the *Jewish Advocate* (October 27), discussing the Arab boycott of American firms that do business with Israel, and ending with the words, "It's time for a change /Vote Kennedy/ and the winning team."

Such was the nature of the appeal to Jewish voters. How effective it was is anybody's guess.

---

[7]New York *Times,* November 5, 1960.

11. THE JEWISH LIBERAL TRADITION

THE consistent liberalism of American Jews has been noted time and again by scholars and politicians. Jews tend to be equally liberal on political, economic and social matters, whereas workers, for example, tend to be liberal only on economic issues, the educated on political subjects like freedom of speech but not on economic questions, and Negroes on civil rights but not on foreign affairs.[1]

Most Jewish voters in the United States regard themselves as political independents. But in practice Jews during the last forty years or so have tended to vote Democratic rather than Republican. This voting behavior has appeared aberrant, particularly in the last two decades, because other Americans in the same socio-economic position have voted mostly Republican.

American Jews today are predominantly native. Their incomes are mostly in the middle and upper-middle range; many have college degrees and are self-employed businessmen, proprietors, professionals or managers. More and more of them are adopting a suburban style of life, even though most still live within city limits. In occupation and income, they most nearly resemble Presbyterians and Episcopalians, upper-status Protestant denominations. Similarly situated Protestants and Catholics vote Republican in considerable numbers, and by all the rules, Jewish support of the Democratic party should have declined and withered away. True, during their upward socio-economic passage Jews have trimmed their vote on the Democratic line—witness Great Neck in Long Island and Highland Park outside Chicago. But what is striking is not that Jews in Great Neck vote only 60 per cent Democratic; it is that they vote only 40 per cent Republican.

This display of party loyalty seems to contradict the popular notion that Jews will vote for a Jewish candidate regardless of

---

[1] Cf. Lenski, *op. cit.*, pp. 121-153; Samuel A. Stouffer, *Communism, Conformity, and Civil Liberties* (Garden City, N. Y.: Doubleday & Co., 1955), p. 143 *et passim*. The same phenomenon has been observed among Jews in Amsterdam, England, Australia, Canada and pre-Nazi Vienna. Cf. Seymour Martin Lipset, *Political Man* (Garden City, N. Y.: Doubleday & Co., 1960), pp. 242-244.

party—or Catholics for a Catholic, Italians for an Italian, Negroes for a Negro, and so forth. Actually, this kind of voting reflects the striving of the group for status in society and its need for political recognition.[2] Nearly every ethnic, religious and social group in America, in its drive for power and prestige in the community, has sought public office for its members as tangible evidence of its place in the political body. The more the group needs such recognition, the more likely are its members to vote for "one of their own"—a circumstance to which politicians have traditionally responded with "balanced" tickets. Such political contests among groups, for prestige and sometimes for control of the political machine, occur most frequently in local politics, though occasionally they erupt also on a national scale, the notable examples being the presidential elections of 1928 and 1960.

As issues have grown increasingly complex, many voters have grown more sophisticated and have learned to vote not necessarily for one of their own, but for the candidate who, regardless of faith, color or ethnic origin, seems likeliest to serve their individual, class and group interests.[3] Jews have been especially apt in absorbing this political lesson, and other groups seem to be learning it too.

Jewish voters are probably more influenced by the political stance of a candidate than by his ancestry or religion—at any rate in national elections—because they view politics more ideologically than other groups. Even in municipal elections, where voting for "one of our own" is most common, Jewish voters usually support the Democrat who is not a Jew over the Republican who is, at least in places where they are not hungry for political prestige. For example, in New York's mayoral primary in 1961, 63 per cent of the voters in 23 predominantly Jewish election districts in Brooklyn voted for the reform Democrat, Robert F. Wagner, a Catholic of German-Irish background, while only 37 per cent

---

[2]See Rischin, *op. cit.,* pp. 3-12.

[3]Cf. John Slawson, "Guidelines," [American Jewish] *Committee Reporter,* October 1960, p. 7: "Each voter is the judge of his own interests and if he believes these include religious, racial or ethnic factors, as well as a host of others, his vote may reflect that belief. It is no less legitimate to vote as an American of Greek origin interested in liberalizing the immigration quota for Greece, than as an importer interested in lowering the tariff on foreign textiles."

voted for his Jewish opponent, Arthur Levitt, the regular Demo-crat.[4] In the election proper, Jewish voters once again backed Wagner substantially against the Republican and Jew, Louis J. Lefkowitz.

Another example was the mayoralty election of 1945, when Jewish voters overwhelmingly backed William O'Dwyer, an Irish Catholic Democrat, against his Republican opponent, Jonah J. Goldstein. This has been a recurrent pattern in New York City since 1903, when Jewish voters failed to support Cyrus L. Sulz-berger, running for Borough President of Manhattan on a Repub-lican-Fusion (reform) ticket, and voted instead for his Democratic opponent John S. Ahearn, not a Jew.

The untypical character of Jewish voting has been the subject of considerable analysis and speculation among politicians and students of politics. In 1948 a study of voting among eight religious groups (Baptists, Lutherans, Methodists, Episcopalians, Presby-terians, Congregationalists, Roman Catholics and Jews) showed that on politico-economic questions, groups low in class and status were liberal and groups high in class and status conservative. But the Jews were an exception: though high in class, they nevertheless remained politically liberal. In spite of their economic interests, their feelings as Jews seemed to have determined the way they voted. The authors speculated that Jews felt insecure because they were not fully accepted by high-class ingroups, and that this in-security forced them to identify with outgroups, that is, low-class groups.[5]

A more elaborate interpretation along these lines was based on the political experience of a Philadelphia Jewish banker who had made his fortune in real estate.[6] Early in his career he associ-ated himself with the Republican party and at the 1928 Republican

[4]"The Mayoralty Primary in New York City, September 1961," unpub-lished memorandum, The American Jewish Committee, September 27, 1961.
[5]Wesley and Beverly Allinsmith, "Religious Affiliation and Politico-Eco-nomic Attitude: A Study of Eight Major U. S. Religious Groups," *Public Opinion Quarterly*, XII (1948), 386-388.
[6]James Reichley, *The Art of Government: Reform and Organization Poli-tics in Philadelphia* (New York: The Fund for the Republic, 1959), pp. 72-75.

National Convention seconded the nomination of Herbert Hoover. Shortly thereafter, in the crash of 1929, the bankers of Philadelphia—Republicans all—banded together to meet the crisis, but failed to include the Jewish banker and even denied him help. After that he turned to the Democratic party. This experience in the early 1930's was summed up as an example of the position of Jews in politics:

> . . . The Jews, as a commercial class, could never hope for better than second-best out of an alliance with the commercial and financial class of old family businessmen or with the political party that they dominated. The trouble with the Republican party for the Jews . . . is that the front benches are already taken. . . . Under such circumstances, why not ally himself with the party of the industrial wage-earners, the small-time politicians, the uneducated toilers? For abandoning the party of a class that in any case will not have him, he is rewarded with front seats on the bandwagon of the "party of the little man" when it rolls into power.[7]

A more ideological interpretation of the Jews' political position is that "Jewish liberalism" took shape when Franklin D. Roosevelt began to formulate the New Deal. In the light of their European experience, this theory holds, Jews saw in the New Deal a liberalism which they construed as the political opposite of the right, whose extreme was fascism.[8]

Still another explanation is that traditional Jewish values, rooted in the religious culture, have affected political behavior. *Tsedakah* (charity), love of learning and rejection of asceticism are thought to have molded the political outlook of Jews, as has their constant sense of identification with persecuted minorities.[9]

Undoubtedly all these factors have played larger or smaller roles in making Jews politically liberal. Their European heritage and their political experiences in the pursuit of emancipation, which Werner Cohn analyzes in some detail, may have been the

---

[7]*Ibid.*, p. 74.
[8]Werner Cohn, "The Politics of American Jews," in Marshall Sklare, ed., *The Jews: Social Patterns of an American Group* (Glencoe, Ill.: Free Press, 1958), pp. 622-626.
[9]Lawrence H. Fuchs, *The Political Behavior of American Jews* (Glencoe, Ill.: Free Press, 1956), pp. 175-200 *et passim*.

most significant. With the French Revolution, when the attainment
of political equality became the goal of enlightened Jews, support
of Jewish enfranchisement became part of the program of non-
Jewish liberals and revolutionaries throughout Western Europe. As
Jews gradually won their political rights in Western countries, they
found that the liberals and radicals who sought to change society
were their allies, whereas the conservatives and reactionaries who
wanted to keep the system of caste and privilege—the nobility, the
landed gentry, the established churches—were their enemies. In
England, for example, it was the Archbishop of Canterbury who
rallied the House of Lords to prevent seating a Jew in Parliament
and thus to preserve the Christian character of the state. The
constant opposition of the conservatives to Jewish equality drove
the Jews into the opposite camp. Disraeli long ago said that "the
persecution of the Jewish race has deprived European society of an
important conservative element." [10]

As the struggle for emancipation moved eastward it became
more intense, because social, political and economic conditions in
the Hapsburg empire and in Czarist Russia were more desperate
than in Western Europe. Russia was the outstanding example of
despotism, autocracy and oppression. Most of Europe's Jews suf-
fered under the rule of the Czars, and most of the Jewish immigrants who began to come to America in large numbers during
the 1880's were from the Czarist empire. The political concepts
they brought with them molded their political views in America,
and the explicitly ideological attitude of many Jews toward
American politics may be a product of that European experience
and outlook. It was an ethnocentric outlook, to be sure, common
to most minorities; good and bad in political life were assessed
largely in terms of the different parties' attitudes toward Jews. As
outcasts of Czarist society, they considered themselves a people
apart from the Russians, and wherever they had the vote they
favored Jewish parties, which addressed themselves primarily to
the situation of Jews rather than the country's general problems.

The Jewish experience in the Russian and Austro-Hungarian

---

[10]Benjamin Disraeli, *Lord George Bentinck: A Political Biography* (New
York: E. P. Dutton, 1905), p. 324.

empires established even more emphatically what Jews had learned in Western Europe: that the political right was at best conservative, avowedly Christian, and committed to the preservation of ancient privileges; it could, and often did, become reactionary and anti-Semitic. The left was either moderate—favorable to change in the established order, opposed to anti-Semitism and often neutral in matters of religion—or revolutionary, anti-clerical, and committed to the overthrow of the social and economic system that had brought little besides poverty and persecution to Jews.

Small wonder, then, that many Russian Jews sympathized with the opponents of the Czarist regime. Certainly their position in Czarist society seemed so hopeless that only a truly radical change could redeem them: general revolution or total emigration, whether to the golden land of America or to Palestine.[11] Thus Jews, moderate and conservative in operating their own communal institutions, came to sympathize with the non-Jewish liberals and radicals who wanted not merely to reform the political order in Russia, but to remake it. The situation was clear to all who could see it. In 1903 Pahlen, the governor of Vilna, wrote in a confidential memoir about the Bund, the Jewish Social-Democratic organization:

> . . . this political movement is undoubtedly a result of the abnormal position of the Jews, legal and economic, which has been created by our legislation. A revision of the laws concerning the Jews is absolutely urgent, and every postponement of it is pregnant with most dangerous consequences.[12]

Jews, then, supported the left, not primarily because they were exploited as workers or oppressed like peasants, but because they were a persecuted minority. This political outlook was characteristically East European. The German Jewish immigrants of the previous generation had had a somewhat different political experience. They had come to America during the reaction that followed

---

[11] In his autobiography, *Trial and Error* (New York: Harper & Brothers, 1949), p. 13, Chaim Weizmann writes about his pious mother, to whom the various modern Jewish ideologies were quite alien: "She would say: 'Whatever happens, I shall be well off. If Shemuel [the revolutionary son] is right, we shall all be happy in Russia; and if Chaim is right, then I shall go to live in Palestine.'"

[12] Quoted in Paul Miliukov, *Russia and Its Crisis* (New York: Collier Books, 1962), p. 364.

the 1848 revolution. In Germany the struggle for emancipation had seemed possible within the framework of the existing society, and Jews by and large had felt committed to that society, provided it made room for them. In the revolution Jewish leaders had fought for the individual rights of Jews as German citizens differing from their neighbors only in religion—a matter which they felt ought to make no difference to their civic status. This opinion was shared by many of the German liberals who played leading roles in the 1848 revolution.

Disappointed by the reaction after 1848, German Jews migrated to America together with other German liberals and followed the German pattern of settlement in the Middle Atlantic states, the Middle West and the West. Active participants in the German immigrant community, they often shared the political outlook of their Christian compatriots. The liberalism of Lincoln's Republican party attracted them, though comparatively few Jews were passionate abolitionists. Even Isaac Mayer Wise, who was to become a Copperhead and Democrat, at first was sufficiently interested in the Republican party to attend its Ohio organizing meeting. He withdrew because non-Jewish German atheists in Cincinnati were too closely identified with the party for his taste.[13] Despite his sympathy for the Confederacy he came to be one of the numerous Jews who admired and loved Lincoln not only for his acts on behalf of Jews but also for his great qualities of heart and mind. This admiration for Lincoln was what enabled many Jews to remain Republican and vote for General Grant in 1868, despite well-founded charges of anti-Semitism against him.[14]

In time, the German Jewish immigrants flourished; many who had started as peddlers became prosperous businessmen and some even merchant princes. They remained almost uniformly loyal to the party because of its business outlook and its conservative fiscal and tariff policies. There was, in fact, hardly any other choice for the politically liberal middle-class voter in the second half of the nineteenth century. The Democratic party, at that time, could

---

[13]Bertram Wallace Korn, *American Jewry and the Civil War* (Philadelphia: Jewish Publication Society of America, 1951), p. 256.
[14]*Ibid.*, pp. 128-137.

not have appealed to him; even when not actually split, as it often was, it was riddled with factions—torn between economic radicalism and conservatism, pulled apart by regional differences among the agrarian populists in the Midwest and West, the agricultural conservatives in the South, and the immigrant groups in the East.

To the East European immigrants, streaming into the squalid ghettos of the industrial cities, the Democratic party looked quite different. They viewed it from their position among the poorest, most sweated, exploited and submerged proletariat of the rapidly expanding industrial system. True, the competition between Democrats and Republicans did not fit their old-country concept of a left-vs.-right polarity. That ideological outlook found expression instead in radical parties, largely transplantations from Europe, which occasionally attracted a significant proportion of the Jewish immigrants' vote. But the Democratic party performed a vital function for the immigrant: however corrupt and greedy, it was often the chief mediator between him and the larger society. The ward heeler and the local boss could help in misunderstandings or disputes with the police, the landlord, the "authorities." [15] All the party wanted in return was a vote, and immigrant Jews were among those who provided the votes. Morris Hillquit describes an area inhabited almost entirely by Jewish immigrants from Russia— the 9th Congressional District on New York's East Side, where he ran unsuccessfully as the Socialist candidate for Congress in 1906: "Geographically it is located in the slums; industrially it belongs to the sweating system; politically it is a dependency of Tammany Hall." [16]

If Jews tended to vote mostly Democratic in those early days, it was not merely out of mistaken loyalty to the local machine. The Democrats were also the pro-immigration party, and immigration was a subject of considerable interest to Jews. In the last decades of the century, the Republican party was essentially nativist, favor-

---

[15]Richard Hofstadter, *The Age of Reform: From Bryan to F.D.R.* (New York: Vintage Books, 1960), pp. 182-185.
[16]Morris Hillquit, *Loose Leaves from a Busy Life* (New York: Rand School Press, 1934), p. 108.

ing restrictions on the admission of aliens.[17] Later, when even the Democrats could no longer resist restrictionist pressure, the Republicans clamored still more loudly for closing America's gates.

There were exceptions to this voting pattern, however. If a Republican candidate was clearly pro-Jewish or responsive to some Jewish need, the immigrants gave him their votes.[18] For example, Jews supported Theodore Roosevelt in 1904, no doubt because in 1902 his Secretary of State, John Hay, had issued a strong note to Rumania condemning mistreatment of Rumanian Jews, and the following year both Hay and Roosevelt himself had denounced the Kishinev pogrom.

The third parties—Socialist, Socialist-Labor and Progressive—attracted substantial numbers (though never a majority) of Jewish voters when the major-party choice was between an agrarian populist Democrat and a conservative Republican, a choice without meaning for the Jewish industrial proletariat, whose estimate of social justice was based on how Jews and urban workers were treated. Among Socialist candidates, the voters distinguished between those who identified themselves with their interests and those who did not.[19]

The ideological, as against the pragmatic, attraction of the Democratic party for Jewish voters all over the nation emerged with Alfred E. Smith's candidacy in 1928. Usually this attraction is thought to have been created by Franklin D. Roosevelt, first with the New Deal and later with anti-Nazism. But in actual fact Roosevelt seems to have merely reinforced an attachment which had been in the making throughout Smith's four terms as Governor of New York (1919-20, 1923-28).

Smith has been called the first Democratic candidate to speak

---

[17]John Higham, *Strangers in the Land* (New Brunswick, N. J.: Rutgers University Press, 1955), pp. 97-105; Maldwyn Allen Jones, *American Immigration* (Chicago: University of Chicago Press, 1960), pp. 261-262.

[18]At the turn of the century the middle-class response to the "shame of the cities" expressed itself in the municipal reform movement. Largely drawn from the ranks of Republicans, the movement was often able to attract high-minded Democrats, too, appalled by the corruption of local Democratic machines. An outstanding example was Cyrus L. Sulzberger.

[19]Cf. Arthur Gorenstein, "A Portrait of Ethnic Politics: The Socialists and the 1908 and 1910 Congressional Elections on the East Side," *Publication of the American Jewish Historical Society*, L (1960), 202-238.

on behalf of the workers in an industrial society.[20] Brought up in a New York slum, trained in politics in the state legislature and the Tammany machine, he rounded out his education by confronting the explosive problems of industrial urban life. He saw that Tammany's Christmas baskets and Fourth of July picnics were no answer to child labor or to disasters like the fire at the Triangle Shirtwaist factory. He was quick to learn from social workers and investigating commissions, and became a pioneer in social legislation.

When Smith was Governor of New York, more than half of America's Jews lived in New York City. Mostly factory workers and small businessmen, they were increasingly drawn to the Democratic party by its growing concern with the social and economic evils of industrial society. In Al Smith they saw not merely the practical social legislator but also the social conscience, the spokesman for the underprivileged and the downtrodden. He fitted into the European concept of the liberal leader who seeks to change the *status quo* peacefully in ways that will help the Jews. Moreover, though he was not of their religion and ethnic background, the Jews of New York looked upon Smith as a symbol of embattled minorities, including their own—a symbol with which they could identify.

By 1928, when he finally won the Democratic presidential nomination, Smith's attractiveness to urban industrial workers and to religious, ethnic and racial minorities was unmistakable. The old Democrats were not pleased. One wrote that Smith obviously intended to appeal

> to the aliens, who feel that the older America, the America of the Anglo-Saxon stock, is a hateful thing which must be overturned and humiliated; to the northern negroes, who lust for social equality and racial dominance; to the Catholics who have been made to believe that they are entitled to the White House, and to the Jews who likewise are to be instilled with the feeling that this is the time for God's chosen people to chastise America yesteryear [sic].[21]

---

[20]Arthur M. Schlesinger, Jr., *The Age of Roosevelt,* Vol. I: *The Crisis of the Old Order: 1919-1933* (Boston: Houghton-Mifflin, 1957), pp. 95-100.
[21]George Fort Milton of Tennessee to W. G. McAdoo, July 1928, *ibid.,* pp. 126-127.

The campaign of 1928 succeeded in tying the Jewish voters even more closely to Smith than might have been foreseen. The vicious anti-Catholic propaganda deeply reinforced Jewish loyalty to Smith in a way that class interest could not have done. The Rev. John Haynes Holmes, minister of the Community Church in New York, commented:

> What I had in mind about the Jews in this campaign is the fact, which I hold not to their discredit but to their honor, that their hearts leap out in sympathy for a man like Gov. Smith who is suffering under the stripes of persecution which the Jews have borne for centuries, and in admiration for this man's courage in defying bigotry and vindicating liberty.[22]

In all large cities, Jews voted overwhelmingly for Smith.[23] Because Smith spoke unmistakably for the industrial worker in the big city (he broke the Republican hold on the Northern cities, carrying 122 previously Republican counties[24]), and because Jews were largely industrial workers, their support of the Democratic ticket was generally assumed to be based essentially on class interest. Actually, with this election the modern liberal voting tradition among American Jews emerged, in which the class point of view was subordinated to a larger political outlook.

There is no precise way of knowing how much a voter's perception of his situation as a Jew affects his political behavior. It is doubtful whether most Jews consciously think of themselves as Jews when they act politically. Perhaps only the most ethnocentric do so. Most Jewish voters who support a liberal party or candidate probably justify their position intellectually by explaining that a liberal program extends more benefits to more people than a conservative program, and is more likely to lead to a good society where it is individual merit rather than family, race or religion that counts. But who can say to what extent these voters explicitly calculate that such a society is inevitably good for Jews, or that in such a society Jews will not be scapegoats? Studies of political behavior are not yet refined enough to tell us how much and in what way submerged or subconscious insecurities affect rational

---

[22]*Jewish Daily Bulletin,* October 30, 1928.
[23]Fuchs, *op. cit.,* pp. 66-67.
[24]Lubell, *op. cit.,* pp. 34-35.

political decisions and color political motivations. In any event, this widespread feeling about the good society which we have come to identify as Jewish liberalism first began to express itself in the support for Al Smith in 1928.

With Roosevelt's accession and his New Deal program, American politics took on a character which Jews had no difficulty in recognizing as distinctly European. The New Deal reforms made the image of the Democratic party created by Smith appear ideologically even more appealing. Left and right were now clearly discernible. In addition, Jews were particularly susceptible to Roosevelt's charisma—witness Republican Judge Jonah J. Goldstein's pun: "The Jews have three *velten* [worlds]: *di velt, yene velt* [this world, the next world] and Roosevelt."

In 1940, when fears of intervention in Europe's war stirred isolationism and opposition to Roosevelt, Jewish voters became even more firmly rooted in the Democratic party. On the eve of the election, one report to Roosevelt stated that in New York only the Jews were solidly for him.[25] By 1944, when America was deeply involved in the war, political alignments were shifting decisively and the Roosevelt coalition began to break up; but the Jews stood firm. They remained Democratic even in 1948, except for a modest defection to Henry A. Wallace, the Progressive candidate.

Jewish voting since 1928 has paralleled the pattern of voting in industrial urban areas where working-class immigrants and their children have predominated. But in the 1930's the occupational composition of American Jews began to undergo substantial changes. The second generation, better educated than their immigrant parents, were then taking on white-collar jobs, entering government service, and becoming professionals,[26] though widespread unemployment and the prevailing poverty of the depression partially obscured the extent of the occupational transformation. Observers during this period erroneously took economic factors to be the main reason why Jews supported the Democratic party. A

---

[25]James MacGregor Burns, *Roosevelt: The Lion and the Fox* (New York: Harcourt, Brace, 1956), p. 453.

[26]Nathan Glazer, "Social Characteristics of American Jews, 1654-1954," *American Jewish Year Book,* LVI (1955), 20-24.

few cited influences other than economic, but on the wrong evidence: they suggested that Roosevelt had solidified the Jews' Democratic loyalties by his appeal as an anti-Nazi. Actually, Roosevelt was far from being a political or ideological pioneer of anti-Nazism; he followed a policy of utmost caution until the tide of public sympathy following the Battle of Britain in 1940 swept him into the interventionist camp.[27] Most Jews did indeed see Roosevelt as an ardent anti-Nazi even in the early days, but in their intense admiration they were attributing their own feelings and views to him.

After the Second World War, the economic and occupational metamorphosis of American Jews became unmistakably apparent. They had shared in the country's rising prosperity. At the start of the 1950's most Jews were in business, white-collar occupations and the professions. Their socio-economic structure now increasingly resembled that of high-status groups who voted Republican, and their continued preference for the Democratic party appeared ever more idiosyncratic. In the 1952 presidential election, the Democratic candidate received about 75 per cent of the votes cast by Jews.[28] No other group in the population—trade unionists, Negroes or young people—supported the party so solidly and consistently. And in 1956, when many other Democratic voters shifted to Eisenhower, the Gallup poll found that 75 per cent of Jewish voters still remained firmly entrenched in the accustomed column.

In the absence of firm data, we can only speculate about the reasons. Jews were greatly attracted to Adlai E. Stevenson, in part because the qualities of urbanity, education and culture which he personified have always appealed to them. But, more important, Stevenson's popularity with Jews was deeply rooted in their political—in fact, ideological—outlook on McCarthyism. Stevenson had been a target of Senator Joseph R. McCarthy's "anti-Commu-

---

[27]Burns, *op. cit.,* pp. 262-263, 397-404.

[28]According to the 1952 post-election surveys by the American Institute of Public Opinion (Gallup), the figure was 77 per cent; the National Opinion Research Center (Roper) found it was 74 per cent and the Survey Research Center of the University of Michigan found it was 73 per cent.

nist" campaigns, which neither the Republican presidential candidate nor the Republican party leadership had repudiated. The images McCarthy conjured up among Jews were frightening: visions of storm troopers goose-stepping down Broadway, of an America taken over by a red, white and blue reincarnation of Hitler's Brown and Black Shirts. The Senator from Wisconsin seemed to symbolize that "it could happen here." However exaggerated their fears, most Jews recognized McCarthy as a demagogue bent on exploiting for his own aggrandizement the nation's abhorrence of Communism and anxiety over Russia. They sensed in McCarthy's anti-Communism qualities similar to Hitler's, though he was not anti-Semitic and even tried to show his philo-Semitism. They feared his cynical opposition to liberalism and his contempt for due process. Many felt threatened in their security not only as American citizens but also as Jews, associating McCarthy with anti-Semitism. Most believed instinctively that no good could come to them from this quarter.

The depth of hostility against McCarthy among Jews has been measured in various surveys. A Gallup poll in June 1954 found intense disapproval among 65 per cent of Jews interviewed, as compared with 31 per cent of Protestants, 38 per cent of Democrats and 45 per cent of college graduates. In March 1957 a Roper poll gauged attitudes toward McCarthy by index numbers; the index for the Jewish group stood at -46, while the group next in line, consisting of executives and professionals, rated only -18.

McCarthy may have pushed Jews toward the Democratic party as much as Stevenson pulled them. Stevenson did not actually hold all the views which many Jews imputed to him. He was, for instance, not an enthusiastic supporter of Israel in the Arab-Israel conflict, though most Jews seem to have taken it for granted that he was. Nor was he as pro-labor as Jews and liberals believed. In 1952, as a generation earlier, the political or ideological, more than the economic, differences between the Republican and Democratic parties determined how most Jews voted. The same was true in 1956 and 1960, when Nixon incurred a good deal of the suspicion Jews had felt about McCarthy. To be sure, the hostility was less intense, yet Nixon's association with ideologically rightist anti-Communism again raised the question, however unwarranted, of anti-Semitism.

Political traditions brought from Europe (particularly Eastern Europe), economic experiences among the urban proletariat, and insecurities about anti-Semitism have combined to shape a middle-class American Jewish liberalism that has usually expressed itself at the polls in Democratic voting. This liberalism has become so pervasive that many descendants of German Jewish immigrants, whose fathers and grandfathers were Republicans, have come to vote Democratic in the last two or three decades. By now liberal voting may have become part of a family group tradition—a habit and custom difficult to shed, particularly at that final moment in the voting booth when what Paul Lazarsfeld once called "terminal horror" assails the voter, preventing him from pulling the un-accustomed lever.

Today American Jewish liberalism seems to be sustained largely by this family and group tradition. Its earlier formative elements apparently are fading. European experiences antedating the First World War are remote and unfamiliar to the three-fourths of American Jews who are native-born. Even the recent past of Nazi Germany and the Second World War is a matter of book learning for a new generation. Memories of unemployment and poverty may still linger among the many American Jews who experienced the depression of the 1930's or witnessed the economic hardships of immigrant parents; but such recollections, too, are increasingly becoming part of a distant and even irrelevant past. The decline of overt anti-Semitism, the growing acceptance of Jews in nearly all occupations and at nearly all levels, will also probably affect the political behavior of Jews. If Jews find themselves wholeheartedly accepted, socially as well as professionally, by Gentiles whose class and status have made them Republican, the Jewish political style may change. The identification of the political right with anti-Semitism—an identification based almost exclusively on European politics—may then lose its meaning. Acculturation and full acceptance by Christians may in time deaden or at least dull Jewish sensitivity and feelings of insecurity. When this happens, class interest will probably affect voting more than Jewish group identity. But that time is still in the future.

12. CONCLUDING OBSERVATIONS

THE PRESENT studies amply support the widespread belief that religion was an important factor in the 1960 vote. With the Democratic candidate a Catholic, some Catholic areas voted a little more heavily Democratic than they might have done otherwise, and some Protestant ones a little more heavily Republican. But religion was far from being the only basis of choice; its interplay with economic or class interest, party loyalty, ethnic background and local political conditions was so varied that the conclusions reached in these studies often apply only to particular groups in particular places.

The Persistence of Groups

One distinctive characteristic of these studies is that they take groups seriously. The history of group life in America, particularly since the end of mass immigration soon after the First World War, suggests that for whatever reasons—quite likely because they satisfy affective needs of their members—groups and their traditions will survive long after the explicit purposes they were expected to meet have ceased to exist. In the earlier years of the present century, it may have been reasonable to believe that with the Americanization of the second and third generations the descendants of immigrants would cease to constitute distinct groups, and that the organizations established to deal with the problems confronting immigrants in a new land would prove transitory. But this has not happened; though the descendants of the immigrants have retained little of the distinct cultures their forebears brought with them from abroad, they have nevertheless kept a sense of belonging to their particular groups.

Reflections on this important aspect of American life and history may well be relevant to some of the material in these studies. The predominant political philosophy of the English-speaking countries is individualistic and rationalistic; it understands how individuals can act in their own interest, but is not able to deal with the impact of groups and group traditions. As a result, even intelligent people have seen in the persistence of the "hyphenated

American" little more than a plot of politicians to balance tickets and win votes. Our studies, on the other hand, suggest not only that group traditions and attitudes affected by membership in groups are relevant to voting behavior, but that important aspects of the histories of groups may have been obscured by the dominant rationalist tradition in political theory and study. Thus, much of what was heretofore considered purposive action toward the realization of goals determined by self-interest may have to be interpreted as a reflection of group feeling and tradition.[1] This will be made clearer by some remarks on both New England Yankees and Jews.

In our study of Providence we reported that Yankee voters favored both the Republican candidate for President and the Democratic candidate for United States Senator. In this they were behaving as ethnic minorities are often thought to do, and as their Italian fellow townsmen clearly do. One obvious explanation (though, as we shall see, by no means the only one) is that the Yankees, finding themselves a beleagured minority in New England, which was once theirs alone, are beginning to take on certain characteristics of ethnic minorities—among them that of supporting candidates of their own group. One can easily imagine their thoughts and feelings about an election in which an Irish Catholic Democrat was seeking the presidency, while a French Canadian Catholic ran for the Senate on the Republican ticket. That both parties had nominated Italian Catholic candidates for Governor could hardly be thought to improve matters; here, the ethnic factor being equal, Yankee voters followed their usual inclination and supported the Republican.

The impression that New England Yankees are only now taking on ethnic characteristics may well be due to the perspective in which they have usually been viewed in relation to later immigrants. Newcomers, it was thought, or at any rate their children

---

[1]This is not to say that all members of a group are equally affected by its political tradition. That class and status factors may be involved in susceptibility to group influence is suggested by the stronger pro-Kennedy deviation in the Irish Catholic middle-class ward studied in Buffalo than in the lower- and upper-class areas.

and grandchildren, would become assimilated to an America destined to remain fundamentally Anglo-Saxon. In this context the Yankees, as descendants of colonial settlers and Revolutionary warriors, appeared to be the very antithesis of an ethnic minority. One consequence of this supposed antithesis was that the organizations of the early settlers' posterity were commonly known as "patriotic" societies, while those of the later immigrant groups were considered as "hyphenated American." Yet both apply exactly the same kind of genealogical criteria for membership—which might lead us to wonder whether the so-called patriotic societies should not be seen as essentially Anglo-American ethnic organizations.[2]

The reason the descendants of the earliest immigrants have not been considered as an ethnic group is that such groups have been habitually viewed as embodiments of separate cultures and ways of life, destined to merge with the surrounding Anglo-American society once their distinctive culture was lost. But, as we have noted, this has not happened; ethnic-group identity is surviving even in the absence of ethnic culture. We must recognize, therefore, that criteria for distinguishing between groups need to be revised, and that we should place emphasis upon feeling and affective elements rather than overt ones like language. All this suggests that group consciousness, far from being transitory or socially pernicious—as suggested in Rousseau's *Social Contract*—is entirely normal and reasonable. A re-examination of the history of the Yankees from this viewpoint might prove revealing.

Our examination of Jewish voting points to still another way in which emphasis upon individual (for the most part economic) self-interest has blinded us to the importance of group traditions and made them appear politically aberrant. As we have noted, the voting behavior of Jews in recent decades has seemingly run counter to their social and economic condition. In the

---

[2]The term would have to be used broadly enough to encompass non-English early settlers—notably the Dutch—who became assimilated to the Anglo-American group and its ideals, and whose descendants are accepted by the "patriotic" societies. This assimilation was far advanced by 1836, when Martin Van Buren was elected eighth President of the United States.

early part of this century, this was not so. Most Jews then belonged to the lower-income strata, and many worked in sweat-shops; thus, their preference for liberal or even radical candidates seemed entirely in keeping with reasonable self-interest. Students of politics have found this shift away from apparent self-interest rather perplexing.

The details of this development have been presented in the preceding chapter. We need not repeat them here, but one implied lesson may be underscored: Matters of this kind may seem per-plexing only because of the assumptions we bring to them—the individualistic assumptions of conventional political philosophy with its strong emphasis on economic self-interest. The rise of a politically liberal tradition among Jews, in consequence of their historical experiences in modern times, becomes perfectly under-standable if we keep these presuppositions from intruding.

Third Groups

Rivalry and competition among ethnic groups are a familiar aspect of American life and history. The conflicts likely to arise when a group seeks to win a place for itself or for its members in American society have been widely noted by scholars. But not enough attention has been paid to another phenomenon of inter-group relations: the effect of third groups. We have observed this effect, at least in passing, in Louisiana, where Negroes con-stituted the third group, and in suburban Detroit, where Jews did. No doubt other instances exist, particularly in multi-ethnic areas; a study of these might well yield results interesting to historians and political scientists.

The settings in our two cases are quite different. In suburban Detroit the conflict was between Catholics and Protestants. If one of the hypotheses offered in our discussion is correct, the presence of the Jewish third group affected the other two groups' per-ception of the political situation, enabling both to see that Ken-nedy was not "the Catholic candidate," and neutralizing the religious issue with its attendant emotionalism.

In Louisiana the conflict involved racial, political and states'-

rights issues with some overtones of religious differences. The presence or absence of Negroes in considerable numbers seems to have had some effect upon how white citizens voted. Because of Southern nervousness in the face of the Negroes' vigorous demands for equality, the effect of the third group in this case was to increase the stress.

It is worth noting that this effect of Negroes as a third group was observed only in parishes where the white residents were predominantly Protestant, not where they were mostly Catholic and of French descent. If we were to account fully for this difference between the two white groups, we might well have to consider elements of group tradition analogous to those discussed above. The existence of such differences confirms us in our view that at the moment more is to be gained from political studies *in situ* than from simple extensions of findings in one place or about one population to other places and populations. Thus, in the present instance we cannot talk about the effect of Negroes upon white voters in Louisiana generally; we must specify which white voters we mean.

Variations in Group Voting

Students of American voting behavior all too frequently have looked upon religious, ethnic and other groups as more or less homogeneous categories of voters. Thus, it has seemed significant that this or that percentage of Catholics (or Negroes, or workers, or college graduates) voted for this or that candidate or party. Now, any population count assuredly will yield some determinate cardinal number, and any ratio can be computed as a specific percentage; but whether such data are always politically informative is quite another question. We expressed doubts on this point before, and a glance at some of our findings underscores these doubts.

Broad statements about the Protestant vote are surely pointless. No one will be surprised to find the varieties of American Protestantism with their manifold ethnic and cultural associations reflected in variegated voting behavior. Both Lutherans in Minnesota and Fundamentalists in Tennessee are Protestants; yet, at least in the areas we studied, the former were almost untouched by the religious issue and the latter very much affected.[3]

General pronouncements about other religious and ethnic groups turn out to be equally ill-founded. We studied Italian voters in two neighboring cities—Boston and Providence—in which they are numerous, and found their voting habits noticeably different. It seems that in Boston a candidate's Italian ancestry is rather less of an attraction for his fellow ethnics than in Providence— which is not to say, of course, that Boston Italians are wholly unsusceptible to the pleas of Italian office-seekers. Thus, it appears that a simple statement even about "the Italian vote"—a term with a more clearly delineated reference than "the Catholic vote"—would not be really informative.

As a final example we may cite the Negro vote. Press reports before and after the election indicated that Negroes all over the country strongly preferred Kennedy and the Democratic party. Yet, as we have seen, this was not so in Boston or in rural Tennessee. True, it might be said that a high percentage of Negro voters supported Kennedy, *other things being equal*. But unless we can say which things were equal and which unequal, that statement means only that most were for Kennedy and some not. We need to know just why the minority voted as it did. Once we know the varied factors which led different groups of Negroes to vote in different ways, the original simple generalization about Negro voting no longer has any point.

*   *   *

If our experience in the present book has made us reluctant to extend our findings beyond their original locales and conscious

---

[3]Since Germans, Scandinavians and Irish are all of the Old Immigration, it has been suggested to us that the Minnesota Lutherans, who might have been expected to oppose Kennedy's candidacy on religious grounds, favored him because a President who was not a descendant of colonial settlers would symbolize the equality of Old Immigrant with Old Stock Americans. Conversely, the Tennessee Fundamentalists, themselves Old Stock, may have opposed Kennedy not only on religious grounds but also in order not to have to acknowledge this equality. For want of actual evidence, one can only speculate, but if there is anything at all to this, then Old Immigrant and Old Stock American may be more relevant political categories than Protestant and Catholic, though not likely more than Irish Catholic and Italian Catholic.

of how frequently the outcome of an election is affected by purely local conditions and events which are easily missed when attention is not focused on them, we realize nevertheless that much of what we have written is suggestive beyond the limits of the study itself. It is not so much that we may have stumbled upon answers to questions asked by others; rather, our findings may suggest further questions which can be answered only by further research.

INDEX

(The names of John F. Kennedy, Richard M. Nixon, Dwight D. Eisenhower, Adlai E. Stevenson and of the Democratic and Republican parties have not been indexed.)

Ahearn, John S., 78

Anglo-Americans: in Buffalo, 16; in Louisiana, 49-50. *See also* Yankees

Anti-Catholicism, 41-48, 52-55, 68-70, 86

Archambault, Jr., Raoul, 31, 33, 34

Baptists: in Tennessee, 42; in downstate Illinois, 42-43. *See also* Fundamentalists

Bender, George H., 23

Bricker, John W., 23, 25

Brooke, Edward W., 14-15

Brothers, A. S., 14

Brown, Edmund S., 36, 37

Cape Verde Negroes: *See* Negroes in Providence

Catholics: in Boston, 9-11; in Buffalo, 16-21; in California, 35; in Cincinnati, 22-27; in Detroit, 66; in Harper Woods, Mich., 68-69; in Minnesota, 55-58; in Oak Park, Mich., 68-70. *See also* French Canadians, French Catholics, German Catholics, Irish, Italians, Poles

Celeste, Vincent J., 9

Celler, Emanuel, 74

Curtis, Lawrence, 74

Del Sesto, Christopher, 31, 33, 34

DiSalle, Michael V., 23, 25, 48

Ethnic groups, 91-94. *See also* specific names

Ewing, Bayard, 32

Farmers, 51-58

Ferguson, "Jumping Joe," 25

Forand, Aimé J., 31

Freeman, Orville L., 54-55, 57-58

French Canadians in Rhode Island, 31

French Catholics in Louisiana, 49-50

Fundamentalists: in Shreveport, La., 50; in southern Illinois, 46; in Tennessee, 42, 96. *See also* Baptists, Methodists

Furcolo, Foster, 10

German Catholics: in Cincinnati, 23-24; in Clinton County, Ill., 27

German Lutherans: in Buffalo, 17; in Chicago, 62-64; in Minnesota, 51. *See also* Germans, Lutherans, Protestants

Germans: in Buffalo, 16; in Chicago, 61-64; in Cincinnati, 22-23

Goldstein, Jonah J., 78, 87

Gore, Albert, 41

Hay, John, 84

Hillquit, Morris, 83

Holmes, John Haynes, 86

Humphrey, Hubert H., 54, 55, 58

Irish: in Boston, 9-11; in Buffalo, 17, 92; in Chicago, 61; in Cincinnati, 22; in Providence, 28-29, 34

Italians: in Boston, 9-12; in Buffalo, 16, 17; in Cincinnati, 22; in Providence, 28-32; voting patterns, 96

Javits, Jacob K., 73
Jews: in Boston, 9-10, 12; in Buffalo, 16; in California, 35; in Chicago, 61-65; in Detroit, 66; in Great Neck, N.Y., 65-66; in Los Angeles, 35-36; in Oak Park, Mich., 67-70; in Providence, 34; socio-economic characteristics, 76; special appeals to, 71-75
Johnson, Lyndon B., 74

Kefauver, Estes, 41
Kennedy, Joseph P., 73
King, Martin Luther, 20
Knight, Goodwin J., 37
Knowland, William F., 37

Lausche, Frank J., 23, 25, 48
Lefkowitz, Louis J., 73, 78
Levitt, Arthur, 78
Lewis, Dean J., 31
Lodge, Henry Cabot, 9, 74-75
Lubell, Samuel, 3
Lutherans: in Minnesota, 51-55, 95-96; in southern Ohio, 46. See also German Lutherans, Scandinavians

McCarthy, Eugene, 55, 57-58
McCarthy, Joseph R., 88-89
McDonald, David J., 19
McGrath, J. Howard, 30, 34
Methodists: in southern Ohio, 46-47; in Tennessee, 42

Mexicans in Los Angeles, 35-37
Monosson, Fred, 75

National Association for the Advancement of Colored People, 13
Negroes: in Boston, 12-15; in Buffalo, 16, 17, 19-20; in Cincinnati, 22, 23-26; in Detroit, 66; in Fayette and Haywood counties, Tenn., 15; in Los Angeles, 35-37; in Louisiana, 49-50; in Providence, 28-32; variations in group vote, 96
New England Yankees. See Yankees
Notte, Jr., John A., 29, 32, 33, 34

O'Connor, Jr., Thomas J., 10
O'Dwyer, William, 78
O'Neill, C. William, 25

Pastore, John O., 32
Peabody, 3rd, Endicott, 34
Pearson, Drew, 74
Pell, Claiborne de B., 29-30, 32, 33, 34
Poles: in Buffalo, 16-20
Pollard, Rev. Ramsay, 42
Prohibition, 47
Protestants: in California, 35; in Harper Woods, Mich., 68, 69; in Louisiana, 49-50; in Oak Park, Mich., 67-70. See also Baptists, Fundamentalists, Lutherans, Methodists, Yankees

Radziwill, Prince Stanislas, 17
Rhodes, James A., 25
Roberts, Dennis J., 30, 31-32, 34

Roosevelt, Franklin D., 46, 52, 54, 57, 79, 84, 87-88
Roosevelt, Theodore, 84

St. Germain, Fernand J., 31
Saltonstall, Leverett, 13
Scandinavian Lutherans in Minnesota. *See* Lutherans
Scandinavians in Chicago, 61-64
Smith, Alfred E., 42, 44, 46-47, 52, 57, 84-87
Socio-economic groups: in Boston, 10-12; in Buffalo, 20-21; in Cincinnati, 23-27; in Providence, 29, 32-34; in Louisiana, 50. *See also* Farmers, Union members
Southern Baptist Convention, 42, 44
States' Rights party, 42, 50
Sulzberger, Cyrus L., 78, 84

Taft, Robert A., 25
Thurmond, Strom, 15, 42
Truman, Harry S., 42, 46, 48, 54, 57

Union members, 19-21, 67

Volpe, John R., 13, 34

Wagner, Robert F., 77
Wallace, Henry A., 87
Ward, Joseph D., 13, 34
Wise, Isaac Mayer, 82
Workmen's Circle, 61-62

Yankees in Boston: 9-12; in Massachusetts, 34; in Providence, 28, 33-34; considered as ethnic group, 92-93
Young, Stephen M., 48